The Abuela Stories Project

Peggy Robles-Alvarado
Daisy Arroyo

The Abuela Stories Project

Copyright © 2016 Peggy Robles-Alvarado

All rights reserved. No part of this book may be reproduced, stored in a retrieval system, or transmitted in any form by any means, whether electronic, mechanical, photocopied, recorded, or otherwise, without written permission of the author.

ISBN: 978-0-9832777-2-9

Concept and editing by Peggy Robles-Alvarado
Photography by Daisy Arroyo
Cover and Layout by Carmelo Dominguez - vginyc.com
Proofreading and additional edits by Bernice Sosa,
Denise Dominguez and Yoseli Castillo Fuertes

This publication is made possible with public funds from
the Bronx Council on the Arts
through the Department
of Cultural Affairs' Greater New York Arts
Development Fund Program
and through Robleswrites Productions

Dedicación

The Abuela Stories Project is inspired by and dedicated to
Ibaye Mamá Lolita Ana Dolores Acosta de Dominguez,
Ibaye Dolores Ocasio Ortega de Robles,
Ibaye Papi Pedro Robles - Love you all the way!

    Mami Maria Dominguez de Robles - La Gloria y fuerza de mi vida,
    Daisy Anglero Torres who serves loves in every dish she cooks,
    Visionary Daisy Arroyo,
    and to the

        Abuelas who demand we call their names,
        Abuelas who want us to find them.

The Abuela Stories Project

El por qué

Grandmother, Nana, Mamá-no matter what term we use to describe them, Abuelas play a pivotal role in our identity, customs, and conditioning through chancletazos, gentle hugs, or vivid memories.

After becoming an Abuela in my thirties and as an act of creative rebellion against those who found little value in stories about these modern day matriarchs, I created The Abuela Stories Project to accentuate and examine this complex familial role through poetry, prose and photography. I wanted to break the limited archetype of the domesticated Abuela sitting in the rocking chair or relegated to a desolate kitchen. I questioned what made this title significant or agonizing and wondered about my own Mamá Lolita whose unexpected death I recall more than any other moment of her life.

I was curious about Mamá Lolita's unexplored passions, guarded intimate moments, tearful regrets, and the life I was not privy to. Her oral narrative was always limited and purified of any bochinche or controversy. But no woman has a singular story. Documented or not, Abuelas have intricate tales or love, loss, wickedness and righteousness. Their presence and absence affect the families they belong to, particularly young girls and women who are part of their kin. Abuela, whether loving or not, becomes a pillar of the family unit, el ejemplo a woman affectionately accepts or vehemently rejects.

In this anthology, intergenerational women writers, at various stages of their careers, were invited to tell of their Abuelas, and to pull from inspiration provided by photographs taken by visual artist Daisy Arroyo of seven models who allowed the camera, poetry, and prose into their distinct and exquisite lives. This collection celebrates the multifaceted, intricate nature of Abuelas and how they influence our words, art and memory. Here Abuela takes center stage in full spotlight, gets her close up and grips the mic.

Contents

Abuela sabe crear
I
Olga Huraira Ayala

Claudia Whittingham - Re(Member) My Name 3
Peggy Robles-Alvarado - Why I Write About Abuela 5
Nia Andino - Lessons in Chiarscuro 7
Bernice Sosa - Home 10
Rebeca Lois Lucret - Me Pintan 12

Abuela sabe vivir
II
Elena Mamarazzi Marrero

Nia Andino - Tambores De Huracanes 17
Bernice Sosa - Mira pa' donde mí 19
Maria Rivas - Cuénteme 22
PaulA Neves - Work 25
Peggy Robles-Alvarado - Baños de lluvia 26
Alexandra Hernandez - La canción 28
Peggy Robles-Alvarado - Mamá Lolita enseña como vivir 33

Abuela sabe perdonar
III
Tamara G. Saliva

Claudia Whittingham - Silence Memory Longing 38
Shamecca Long - Of The Hands 42
Annette Estévez - Anoche viendo vídeo de La Yiyiyi en YouTú con 45
    la abuela que nunca llegué a conocer or
      La Lupe's Voice is a Full-Bodied Feeling
Nia Andino - To My Grandmother's Shadow 46
Bernice Sosa - Manos de La Doña 48
Rebeca Lois Lucret - Resignation Letter 50

Abuela sabe renacer
IV
Two Moons

Peggy Robles Alvarado - Last Rites Haiku 55
Katalina Rodriguez - Coatlicue 57
Karina Guardiola-Lopez - Headaches and Heartaches 60
Claudia Whittingham - She Shifted The Weight 61
Nia Andino - Between Birds and Shadows 63
Vanessa "Nessa" Acevedo - About "Abuela" 64
Alexandra Hernandez - What Abuela Carries 65

Abuela sabe sanar
V
Maggie Castro Stevens

Vanessa "Chica" Ferreira - What Abuela Carried 71
Annette Estévez - This Poem Is An Unfinished Hanging Thing 72
Karina Guardiola-Lopez - Dos Abuelas 74
Rebeca Lois Lucret - We're Still Dying 76
Peggy Robles Alvarado - Infarto: a zuihitsu set to bolero 78
Shamecca Long - After The Heartbreak (To My Daughter) 81

Abuela sabe moverse
VI
Addie Diaz- Siverio

Shamecca Long - Rebound Haiku 87
Peggy Robles Alvarado - In Leticia's Kitchen Drawer 88
Maria Rivas - ¡Basta! 91
Vanessa "Nessa" Acevedo - A Timeline 96
Alexandra Hernandez - Bonita (Monologue For Her Unborn Daughter) 98
Peggy Robles- Alvarado - Consejos That Remind Me I Am Her (Grand) Daughter 99

Abuela sabe luchar
VII
Shihan Candy Warixi Soto

Shihan Candy Warixi Soto - Aquella Abuela	103
Peggy Robles - Alvarado- Memorandum of understanding between a granddaughter and the sabelo-todos	104
Annette Estévez - I Was Supposed to Be My Grandmother's Namesake or A Crown of Twelve Stars	107
PaulA Neves - The Treatment	110
Vanessa "Nessa" Acevedo - Reading Between, Living Beyond	116

Abuela sabe crear

I

Olga Huraira Ayala: *ol-guh, woman of wind, "eye"-YAH-luh Synonym- Ita*

1. Holy, highly creative, imaginative woman who rejects batas and chancletas. 2. In the business of bridging polymer clay with espíritu, risas, and buen humor; see Hecho A Mano. 3. Defines self as a rare form of slightly crazy that keeps her grounded when wanting to run away from home. 4. Keeps baggie of locks from her grandson's first haircut. 5. After years of battling rolos, alisados, and conformist straighteners, made peace with her crown of curls; una mata de melena; cabello de resistencia. 6. Knows prosperity dwells in fingertips. 7. Creación.

Re (Member) My Name
        Claudia Whittingham

We are a mixture of our
grandmother's rituals and the internet.
The witchcraft of change
mixed with the sanctity of ceremonies.
We are the most beautiful art.

We are the dance looking
to remember its name,
(re)connecting to the ground,

We are an image shaped by eyes
that have never seen us.
We dance temporary shelter

This body an archive,
a connection to history,

a journey through the ruins.
I don't want to spend the rest of my life
blaming the ghosts of dead men,
a harvest of desolation.

Not in exile, amidst the ghosts
of dead men,
amidst the presence of absence,
the presence of war still residing
in the air.

Everything has fallen to the ground,
even the earth, but we are still here,

We are not meant to be locked behind
prison bars, stereotypes, the grief of ruins.

our bodies asking to
make space for a revolution / a conversation.

to Re(Member)
our names.

I want to go home.
To feel the stories that
move me forward.

I want to Re(Member)
my name.

Re(Member)ing our names.

Why I Write About Abuela
  Peggy Robles-Alvarado

Because Dolores means pain, grief and sorrow

Because you never genuinely smiled in photos

Because your story should be more than just your eulogy

Because you swallowed every curse that should have tied his ankles and wrists

Because he silenced you long before the first time he lunged for your throat

Because you sang Odilio Gonzales' boleros aloud hoping he would get the message

Because you wish you could have held all twenty four of your children a bit longer

Because you held each of the undeveloped children that slid down your thighs for too long

Because you named all your daughters after saints like Maria and Altagracia hoping to save them

Because I can only recall your voice reciting the rosary

Because I inherited your fractured heart

Because you were born and died May 26 but I question if you were allowed to really live

Because Papi died May 26 and Mami says you held his hand

Because I ask for your blessing every morning

Because Mami is wearing your face now

Because I will one day wear your face

Because my granddaughter will one day wear your face

Because I want to say your name

Because I want to find you

Lessons in Chiaroscuro
 Nia Andino

By age 2,
I learned the sickness of passions over dry avena, fire alarms and glistening gems.

By age 5,
I was helping Guelita name things with it: bloodstone to nurture,
fire opal for magnetism, tiger's eye for illusions.

By age 8,
Guelita showed me how she marked her love,
committing my face to black dust on the kitchen table. I would awaken to myself
already different from yesterday's version of me. Her fingerprints stained my eyes
to the hum of boleros.

> Bésame,
> bésame mucho,
> que tengo miedo a perderte…

> Mi nieta,
> I've sampled my memory of you while your body was wrapped in the sheets of twilight.
> It is by my hand that you live more than once. My loving may not look like others
> but test me on the tone of your lips. The ones I left puckering in stages of charcoal
> and you will see, through you, I let the light in.
>   -These are Guelita's life lessons in chiaroscuro

By age 12,
Guelita taught me how true beauty surfaces through cracked things,
as we sifted through broken shells the ocean had orphaned,
and I am reminded of being birthed through my mother's C-section scar and torn labia.
The sun turns my skin gold when I learn about the tradition of Kintsukuroi,
and how she and my mother turned their bodies into to Japanese broken pottery,
so I could mend them.

By age 15,
Guelita showed me el poder of being impassioned.
How to balance the hardening of things when heated
like making huevos con pegao,
placing sugar on fire
to massage la gripe of corazones shipwrecked in bellies,
and baking clay after molding it
so it can stand firmly on its own.

By age 18,
Guelita taught me how to kill things in small doses
by watching water rust coffee cans,
and paint poison water.
She explained to me how the things around you can stain you.
Her pigmented hands forced the weeping of rags into muddled rainbows,
like a forgotten Easter,
and the dark of my eyes
revealed all her world had colored on me.

Home
    Bernice Sosa

These tired, aching hands recorded
precise chins and poquitos of recipes
inherited: guineitos en escabeche,
tortas de trigo con salsita de bacalao,
viandas y verduras, sorullitos de maíz,
and sopita de hueso.

Pushed strollers, pulled hand carts,
carried baggage along memorized
roads of foot, bus and train routes.
These hands helped raise children,
nurtured sick parents through transition,
clutched sternum in agony. Overworked
and achy, stiff and wrinkled with time,
fingers crooked but swollen with
commitment.

Mira pa' donde mí.
Prove the bend in my knuckles ached
not in vain, but with purpose.
Tu vida empezó mejor que la mía.
No seas bruta con manos feas.
Estudia y aprende:
in protest of hardship.

Hug my palm with yours until heartbeats synchronize.
Show what is left of me, el resultado de mi cosecha.
And when my rhythm goes silent, summon my youth.
Usher her spirit towards freedom and peace
as we soar together.

Me Pintan
    <u>Rebeca Lois Lucret</u>

Me pintan de cocina
Me pintan ama de casa
Me pintan canosa o calva
A veces me tienen un poco de piedad
Y me pintan de pañuelo
Me pintan sin dientes
Me pintan doblada

    Ciega
    Débil
    Loca
    Lenta

Me pintan de bastón
Y batas anchas
El cuerpo ya no existe
Me pintan de árbol
Cada arruga como cada anillo
Acercándome a los últimos años

    Me pintan estrujada
    Y después me toman la foto
    Y lo llaman arte
    Me pintan sin tetas
    o de tetas plachadas
    o de tetas que alcazan las rodillas

Me pintan de hambre
Me pintan sin azúcar

    Sin sólido
    Sin arroz
    Sin dulce

Ni siquiera me dan un chin de sal
Dique la presión

    Me pintan de artritis
    Me pintan mal del corazón
    De cáncer
    De diabetes

Pero sí me pintan eficiente
para cuidar los mocosos

    Me pintan sola
    A veces tengo la familia
    Pero nunca las amistades
    nunca el marido
Resulta que siempre muere primero

Y te pregunto
¿Y es fácil?

Abuela sabe vivir

II

Elena Mamarazzi Marrero: *eh-lehn-ah, mämə -rat-si, mah-rare-ro*
Synonym- Abuela

1. Pionera, poeta, performer, historian of many hoods, retired profesora, and daughter of Helen Claudio Marrero, St. Cecilia's church and El barrio. 2. Possessor of several collections; see vintage cameras, vejigantes, rocks, stones, strange obsessions. 3. Feels cien por ciento Boricua sin español sitting on her tongue. 4. Inked; see Sol de Jayuya, letter M for her father Mario, for Mamarazzi, and Puerto Rican flag as Nuyorican skyline. 5. Lives in full color and sin verguenza. 6. Straddles drums and finds the pra-ca-tá of the spirit con bomba y plena. 7. Vida.

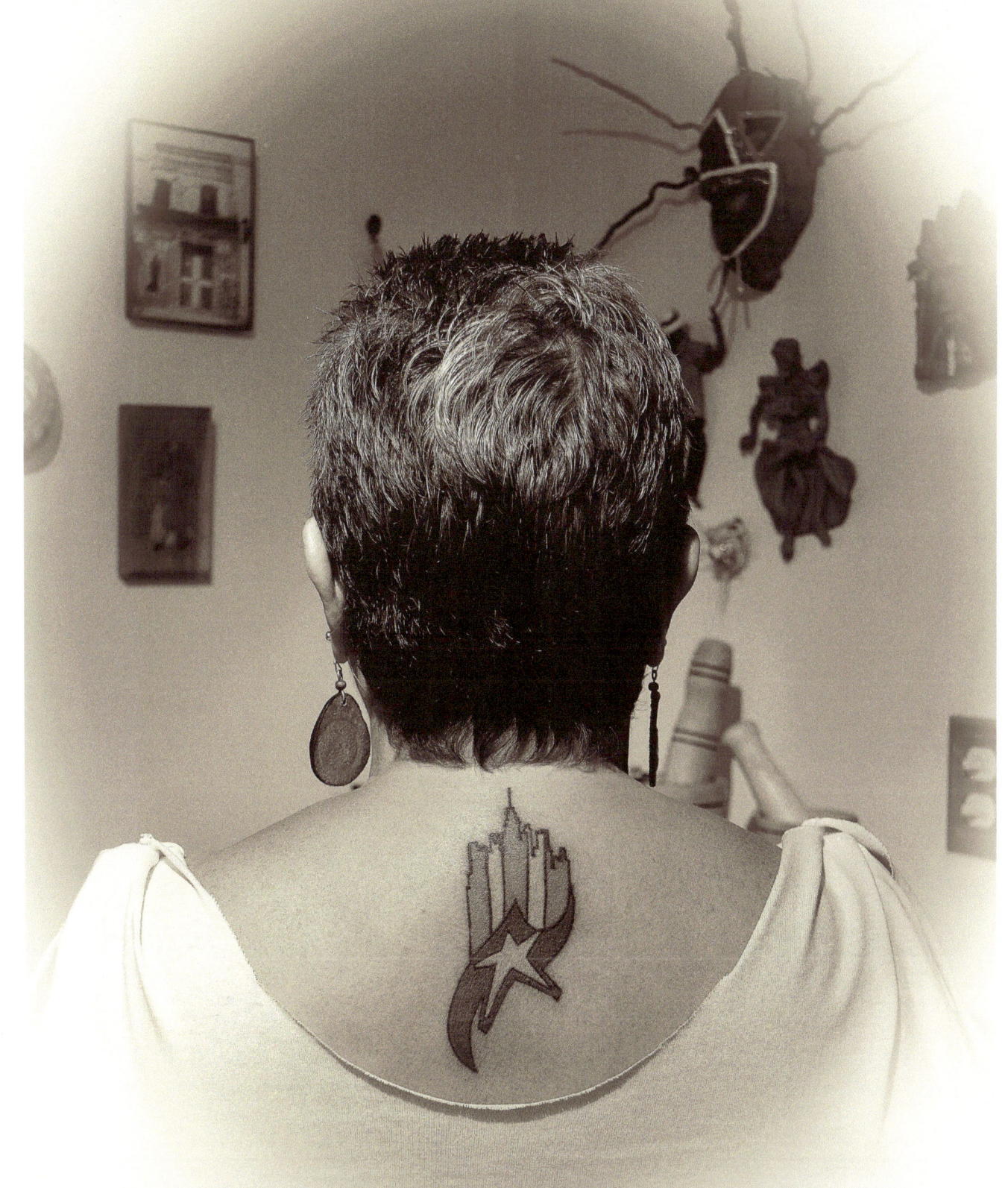

Tambores de Huracanes
    Nia Andino

Abuela said that your heart is your first drum.
It carries rhythm between two lungs
and there is a church inside.
For every prayer that has been silenced,
Abuela remembered being silenced;
                tongue stripped of power,
                      beauty,
                          and accents.

So she escaped with Puerto Rico on her back.
Became huracanes when she couldn't feel it there.
Islands moving across her dented fingernails
until she could see its shape,

and she said
she will be this drum
                until memories stop falling from her eyes,
                    until the mix of 151 and Brut no longer
                        makes her stomach churn,
                            until she could face mirrors again.

And she will be this drum
until she could forget lies knuckled into thighs,
                until the morivivi of hands unclenches her throat,
                  until her past stops trying to deny her
                        la bendición of old age.

Mira pa' donde mí
    <u>Bernice Sosa</u>

1
Mira pa' donde mí. Para que escuches bien lo que te voy a decir.
La vida es una tómbola. No hay nada seguro.
Confía en ti misma y en Dios. Sólo Él sabe lo que hace y por qué.

2
Curious spirit,
Pause.
Rest your head on my lap. Let me caress your fears,
weave calm between ringlets of dry, wild curl.
Let the truth of bent island joints, defeated by
Nueva York winters, leave traces of history upon your
temples and crown. Let them bring you harmony,
soothe ancestral cries. You have great purpose,
mi Paloma, stay aligned.

3
In each groove of my worn, rough hands lies memory;
of carrying water buckets for miles back home to
Quebradillas in drought, of cotton, tobacco, and
rice field afternoons where saved coins replaced
burlap on feet with shoes. These fingers programmed
the signature of my name, the one I could not read
to cross an ocean I could not pronounce
in search of opportunity in belt, hat and glove
factories along Broadway, Nueva York.

Cuénteme
> Maria Rivas

"Cuénteme sus pecados, abuelita. Quiero saber todo."

"Haha, as if I'm going to tell you."

"Come on grandma. I want to carry your dirty little secrets with me. I will put them in a chest of gold, dig a deep hole in my memory where only I have the luxury of knowing. I refuse to believe those rings on your fingers don't have a story to tell. I know those bracelets are bronzed with sweat and tears from the past. I'd like to know where you picked up that 100 year-old Bible that you carry around but never read. You have stories for days and I want to know."

"Everyone has a story."

"Exactly, but nobody has your story. We don't even know how you got to El Bronx!"

"How much do you really want to know?"

"Everything, everything. Todo grandma."

"I will tell you everything but only once. Yo no soy pecadora, soy vividora. That's right, a woman with a life, well lived. Oh, and I lived it, la viví. At fourteen, I chased my prince charming, stole a horse and caught up to him in the darkness. I proposed to him, he accepted. After one year, he left me with your mother in the womb to find work in New York. So, I followed him. We were too poor and he was my prince charming, not Rosa's (my sister). Life in New York was a cold slap in the face! The reality of him with her, the whore and the other whore, numbed my spirit. I got pregnant again, and two more times after that. I taught myself how to drive because I had to. Children force one to take fear and piss on it. Freedom is what I felt when I drove on the highway. So, I decided to become a truck driver. Back then it was not the norm and someone like me, with these red curls and thick hips, was quite a gem. Judgments came from family, neighbors, friends, but they weren't making the money and feeding my children - I was.

"What, you were like Lola the trailera?"

"No, mija even hotter. I had a wicked tongue thanks to New York City. I also packed some rounds thanks to scary gas stations around the states. Every time I returned safely, your grandpa would give me a ring or a bracelet. I wear them with pride! He thought moving to another country would tame me and assumed I would become the holy wife at home. No, mija that was not en mi sangre. And if that's a pecado, then I will accept hell anytime."

"What? That's it?"

"OK. One last thing- just imagine a 24 year old, witty beauty, driving a trailer truck. Yes, it was fun but I still have scars from when it wasn't. That's why I carry this old Bible. I found it on the highway during one of those scary moments. Those stories I will keep in my gold chest, deep in my memory. I'm not a pecadora, mija, I'm a vividora."

Work

    PaulA Neves

Ordering, making change at Burger King,
I didn't cop to knowing "who"
when high school classmates, taunting, ordered fries
again and again, and asked:

"Who's that old bat in the window?
She know you?"

How could she know me
and how could I know
how much plate-glass her palm-framed face
had already looked through?

"Not all work is work," my grandmother had always said,
"Take it from me"

who traveled over 3000 miles
and one rush hour Broad Street intersection
to verify the gravitas of mopping, wiping or simply waiting
had not been lost on me.

Later at home she said, "You pretended not to know me,
but I know you, better than you think."

But what I thought was-
God, I'll be a journeywoman, just like you:

always polishing surfaces,
hoping to find what's underneath.

Baños de lluvia
> Peggy Robles-Alvarado

Mamá's voice is a herald dancing on the cool breeze, pulling the stone colored clouds towards the growing crowd of madres en batas, niños desnudos, viejitos in boxers, all with jabón de cuaba in hand. Along the road we line wide- mouthed barriles, empty soda cracker cans, cubos, and plastic jars ready to collect water that will wash our hair and boil yucca for dinner. Singing to the thunder and lightning severing the sky in a bra and cotton slip, her hair unfettered from a tight bun is a silver shoulder length spiral challenging the thickening sky. Her face, the only inheritance left from an ama de casa and un mujeriego sin rumbo, opens to a toothy smile that narrows both eyes. My wonder woman panties and pink jelly sandals splashing joy against the dirt that swallows the long awaited rain. Weeks of cracked roads and lips slowly softening to mud. Mamá joins the neighbors in cheering on the first drops that play percussion on zinc rooftops. In suds, smiles and song we quickly wash elbows and knees, necks and toes, opening our mouths, dampening the dust
> caught in our throats.

Twenty years later sitting in a Bronx backyard with the cheekbones of an ama de casa and the eyes of a mujeriego sin rumbo, I am stretching overworked limbs across a red plastic lawn chair. Arms and chest opening against a smoke stacked sky. A cotton dress, she would have loved but couldn't afford, fluttering in the swelling wind. I set an empty can of Goya beans by my right foot; an imposter trying to fill the void of a barrio free of zinc rooftops. I close my eyes, rain playing percussion on my arms as cement welcomes the unfamiliar tap of polished toes. The wind cleaning what the water misses as bewildered neighbors shelter under canopies and porches. Opening my mouth, quenching a persistent thirst
> left in her absence.

La Canción
> Alexandra Hernandez

The sound of Abuela shuffling around the upstairs hallway of our house is what brings me out of my sleep. As I lean over my nightstand to grab my cell phone, I rub the sleep out of my sore, tired eyes. The bright screen reads 7:03 AM. It isn't out of the ordinary for my grandmother to be up this early, working and cleaning around the house. I lay back against my pillow and listen to her sounds. She hums an unfamiliar tune, pausing every few minutes to grunt as she grabs something out of the storage closet. I hear what must be a heavy box hitting the floor, as she let out a triumphant sigh.

"¡Dios mío!" she whispers to herself. "So many memories." Then silence again.

I stare up at the ceiling, thankful that it is Saturday and I don't have to get up for school. I daydream about the possibility of practicing new songs on my acoustic guitar, writing down a few song lyrics, or maybe taking a walk to the local library for some books on music. I should also get started on my Christmas shopping. We have three weeks left and (while I have gifts picked for mom, dad and my sister Dee) I still have no idea what to get my grandmother. It's not that she is picky but, every year she insists that we don't need to get her anything. So, year after year, Dee and I present her with things like warm slippers or sweaters from department stores. This year, I want to make it special.

"What are you doing awake so early, mi amor? Did I wake you?" My Abuela stands by the doorway to my bedroom still dressed in her pajamas and a dark red flannel robe. Her glasses are perched on top of her head, grey curly hair sprouting around them like a crown. She smiles at me apologetically. "I didn't mean to be so loud."

"No, no, you weren't," I say, sitting up in bed. "I just couldn't sleep." She nods.

"Want me to make you some coffee? A few pancakes? I already have the batter ready." She knows she doesn't even need to ask. Most days before school, I'm running out of the house with granola bars and a banana but on weekend mornings, Abuela always treats me to a big breakfast. I smile at her and shake my head enthusiastically.

"Absolutely!" She laughs.

"Go wash up and be down in ten." I wait until she makes her way down the staircase before I climb out of bed and walk down the hall towards to the storage closet. When I open it, I see a big cardboard box on the floor. I bend down to peek inside of it. The box is full of old records, a couple of stuffed photo albums and a stack of envelopes tied together with ribbon. I don't recognize the musicians but I take a few out to play on my father's record player in his study later this afternoon.

Next, I pick up the photo albums and I laugh when I see pictures of myself as a toddler. Pictures of myself and Dee at Halloween dressed like Disney Princesses. Pictures from my first recital in the school choir. Pictures of us snuggled up on the couch in my grandmother's old house (the one she shared with Abuelo, before he passed away last year). I hug the albums close to my chest, lost in my own memories. This fall I started applying to colleges, hoping to major in music and I've even had a couple of auditions right before Thanksgiving. It's always been my dream to study music, to write songs that people would hear and fall in love with. But lately, thinking about leaving home and going after this dream has also caused me some fear. I find myself wishing I were still a little girl without a care in the world, aside from getting up in time for Saturday morning cartoons. Everything is changing.

As I start to flip through the second album, I realize that the photos are much older - they're Abuela and Abuelo's wedding photos, photographs of their house when they first bought it, and even some of Abuelo in his Army uniform. Even though it was so long ago, I recognize his shy smile. He was always a big kid, full of laughter and jokes, but he always hesitated to smile in photographs.

"Ay pero, chico, SMILE! Por favor!" I can remember hearing Abuela begging him whenever she tried to take family photos. He would only wink at her and give her the smallest smile he could muster.

Abuela's wedding gown is delicate lace and sepia-toned because of the color of the film. In one of the photographs she is beaming up at him like the queen of the world and he is looking straight at the camera showing off his best Mona Lisa smile. They're beautiful. I miss him. I can only imagine how she feels every day.

Finally, I make my way to the stack of envelopes. They are thin and yellowing in the corners, the ink almost faded. I take a few out of the strings with extra care, making sure I don't mess any of them up. Something tells me if they are in this time machine box then they are important.

"Maria!" Abuela yells up from the bottom of the stairs, startling me from this trip down memory lane. For the first time, I notice that the house is full of delicious smells: bacon, pancake batter, café Bustelo wafting up from kitchen. "Come down, mamita! Breakfast!"

"Okay!" I say, taking a couple of the letters and photos from the box. I stuff them into one of the old records because I want a chance to look through them later. I hope I'm not overstepping by borrowing them because no one has ever shared them with me before. I fold up the box and push it back into its place at the bottom of the closet. I bring the treasures into my bedroom, placing them in my desk drawer for now, and head downstairs for pancakes.

~

Later that afternoon, I manage to get the house to myself. Dee is out with her friends, Dad is on a business trip and Mom took Abuela out for Christmas shopping. I abandon all of my original plans and take the records and letters into Dad's study. I want to listen and read by myself, without interruptions. I place the first record into the vintage record player and bring the needle down. It immediately begins to crackle as a voice fills the room. My grandmother's.

"Mi Amor, Jose. Though you can't be here for the holidays, know that we'll always be together in my heart."

Jose. My Abuelo. When the music begins to play, it is her voice that sings to him, that now sings to us both.

It's a song about longing - about knowing you can't be with the one person you love but continuing to love them and vowing to wait for them anyway. My heart swells at the thought, wondering how it's possible that two people could love each other this much. I always knew they did, (especially after he was gone) but listening to her voice singing for him makes it all click. I didn't even know my grandmother could sing, outside of the Sunday mass. But she really can, and I can't help but wonder why I've never heard it before today. Maybe she kept it as something just for them.

When the song ends, I sit back and take a deep breath in awe. It's one thing to know your grandparents in their old age and through the stories you hear from family members. It's another to see who they were before they sent you birthday cards with ten dollars inside, before they picked you up from school and pushed you on the swings at the playground, before they tucked you in at night. Then I remember the letters. As I hold them in my hand, I decide to choose just one (as much as I would love to read them all). I'm sure it's from Abuelo's time in the Army, the only time they were ever separated, but one letter is enough. The rest are theirs to keep. I pick the envelope with a Christmas wreath stamp and unfold it gently.

Mi Querida Alma,

Merry Christmas Eve. I would say that you have no idea how much I am missing you tonight but after finally having a chance to hear your voice, to hear your song to me, I already know that you do. Tonight, all I can do is remember our summer together, your beautiful face, and pray that this is our last Christmas apart. I don't think that I could handle another. Everyone here is sending packages and letters back to their families and tomorrow we are being treated to a big holiday mass and feast, but it just isn't the same. I can't wait to come back to home to you. For now, I will hold your words close to my heart. Even though I can't be there tonight, you are in my heart.

I love you,
Te amo mucho,
Jose

Tears are streaming down my face as I fold the letter back and place it into the envelope. They were lucky. Not only did they find love but he made it home for every Christmas after that. They made it, together, until he was gone. I wonder if she went looking for this box this morning because she knew this year would be another Christmas apart? I wonder if she wanted to be closer to him? I know I do. Then suddenly I know what I want to give her for Christmas!

~

Over the next couple of weeks, in between classes, or late at night after studying at the local coffee shop with my headphones plugged in, and during any extra time I can find, I play Abuela's song and memorize the lyrics. I was able to record it onto my laptop and now I can carry it around with me. I hum it as I walk down the street and I sing it in the shower when I know she isn't around to hear. I'm learning to play the melody on my guitar.

"What is it that you're always listening to?" Dee asked me one night. We were having a movie night with mom and Abuela but they had fallen asleep on their couch together after the hot cocoa and popcorn were finished.

"Just something I'm working on. For Abuela."

"Can I listen?"

"After I give it to her."

Dee pouted but I didn't want anyone to hear before Abuela heard it. It was my little secret.

~

On Christmas morning, I wake up before everyone else in the house. It is still dark out. The house is silent but cozy. I turn on my desk lamp and write out the card.

To Abuela,

I miss him too but I hope that together, we can keep his memory alive with music.
Merry Christmas. Press play.

Love always,
Maria

I place the card on the dining room table and sit on the staircase, waiting for her to shuffle in early before anyone else rises. It's routine for her to sit by the window, drink a hot cup of coffee and think until we come tumbling into the kitchen as if it were Grand Central Terminal. From my spot on the stairs, I can see her walk in. She's taking her time. She feeds the dog, she makes the coffee. I watch her enjoy a quiet Christmas morning to herself and almost feel like I was intruding by spying, but I want to see her reaction. I want to see what she will say when she presses play. I want so badly to feel it.

Abuela sits down at the dining room table and notices her name on my gifts – the card, an iPod, a few photographs from her albums (me in ballet class, her and Abuelo on a picnic at a beach in Puerto Rico, my favorites from the stack). She smiles as she looks at them, reminiscing. She slides on her reading glasses as she reads my card and plugs the headphones of the iPod into her ears. I watch her squint at the device right before pressing play.

For the last few weeks, I've learned their song inside and out. Not only the lyrics but the melody, adding in my own style along the way and recording it alongside my grandmother's voice. The copy of the song is my Abuela's Christmas present. As she sits at the table, tears stream down her face during her walk down memory lane. My voice guides her, my heart fills with pride. I've spent the last few weeks learning their love, immersing myself in it, hoping one day, I will find the same.

"Maria" she says standing at the bottom of the stairs, eyes bright with tears, "Thank you. Thank you. I didn't think I would ever hear this again, and you made it even more perfect."

"Merry Christmas Abuela." I say wrapping my arms around her and pulling her close. I know one day I'll have to leave, follow my own dreams, but in this moment there is only love. There is only hope.

Mamá Lolita enseña como vivir
Peggy Robles-Alvarado

Within the sterility of scowling bleached walls, doused in unforgiving florescent lights, my body's Caribbean rhythm is losing a battle with the overworked air conditioner humming the tune of a persistent winter. I grip a tissue paper gown at the chest and crotch wishing for hands to hold. Fear and panic sit on my chest in a delirious communion that bullies the air from my lungs as I wait for the doctor.

Trying to find warmth among scalpels, stethoscope, and the blood pressure cuff witnessing my unraveling, I close my eyes and call for Mamá Lolita-the family ambassador to a sacred realm she proved existed beyond faulty bodies and troublesome lab results. She was the mouthpiece to a dimension that needed to be felt before it was seen, a place absent of logic or scientific explanation but saturated with healing.

Calling her name in steady repetition in sync with the mocking heart monitor, the smell of alcohol in the room is triumphed by the aroma of Mamá Lolita's white rebozo; a labor of fingers, lace and cotton, worn to church every Sunday sprinkled in Florida water and camphor. I don't open my eyes. I don't question the feeling; a familiar sentiment she used to spar with death each time she came calling. Death and I have history; tried to claim me her daughter many times with stubborn fevers, indistinct ailments that left the best doctors dumbfounded. But Mamá Lolita was always calling me back, professing me all hers, setting the rebozo over my shoulders as she prayed the rosary, hour after hour, bead after bead, the betrayal of my body her mission, her obra, convincing cells to renew, her voice: a chorus of Dios te salve María dancing with candlelight, the miracle set to soften all that hardened.

The doctor abruptly shuffling through the heavy wooden door jerks me back into the room, my eyes blurred with tears, my shoulders still warm, "Negative, all negative" he declares and I pause a moment before leaping off the table in a holler of gratitude, arms whirling a new set of wings emancipated from my tissue paper gown reaching for Mamá Lolita beyond the white walls, shouting praise to this day and to all the days she teaches me how to live.

Abuela sabe perdonar

III

Tamara G. Saliva: *tuh-mahr-u, jee, sah-lee-vah Synonym - Grandma*

1. Noble, honest, self-made artista, writer, who forgave herself and proved resurrection is possible. 2. Has always refused breaking when immersed in cycles of (re)creation; see Blue Vein Pages and Simples Treasures. 3. Carries her story on her skin, tongue and ori; inked and crowned priestess. 4. Late nights conversing with fate made her believe in second and third chances. 5. Carries a machete for pride and protection, a key for opening and closing paths; hija de oráculo. 6. Believes roots and water can be a tool or weapon of memory. 7. Bendecida.

Silence Memory Longing
  Claudia Whittingham

I

The memory of unspoken words hangs on the edge
slicing the brine from the sea, the salt from tears,
love from our definition of grandmother.
And you wonder…

how I could place my hands around her mouth
and carve her lips into a smile
that is never found in the midst of joy
And you wonder…
why my breasts sag.
My heart's loss hanging in the balance,
I refuse to bend.
My breasts sag
betraying the heaviness of truths
that defy the embrace of words.

                                         And you wonder…
                                         how I can only find other in grandm(other).

II

DNA strewn on barbed wire.
      Almond eyes pierce the shadows
            of a name that doesn't exist on your
                  birth certificate.
                  Vision wandering past the sun.
                      Your father lays in wait,
pressing his weight on your body
        through this barbed wire.
              The symmetry of your silence to his needs
to press his weight on your body.
        You would call your mother's name,
            if you could remember it.
                If she had a phone, or a drum,

                              if she knew you are no longer the little girl
                                        whisked away by your father.

                                  Your mom refused
                 the weight of his pain
                              pressed against hers
                 because your beauty was just enough
                              to remind him that you are his wife's child.

                                  You are the innocence she was until
             his weight pressed against your body,
                      morphing your name,
                              your birthday,
                                   your beauty,
                                        into something
                                              you would never know.

III
Sitting silently, you thought of your Mom.   You miss her.
I think you have missed her   since you were born.

She was fresh cut grass, perfume scented with day old grease,
birthday red roses, green velvet suits, jazz nights, mink coats on frigid evenings.
Waiting on her to make a pit stop between marriages.
Two hours later, you went to bed hungry.   This would be repeated the next month.
Sitting silently, you thought of your Mom.   You miss her.
I think you have missed her   since you were born.

She is unsteady feet on the earth that gave birth to her.
She is the memory of survival trapped in a mind   that yearned for the sun.
She is melting bones   and sagging flesh held together by a diaper.
She never changed your diapers before she left; picking up the dog,
leaving you to the kindness of strangers,   and the comfort of screams.

Sitting silently, you thought of your mom.   You miss her.
I think you have missed her   since you were born.

She is a bundle of bills, the alchemy of a secret that has kept her from
herself…

                                                     Am I my Grandfather's child?

You still miss her.   I think you have missed her   since you were born.

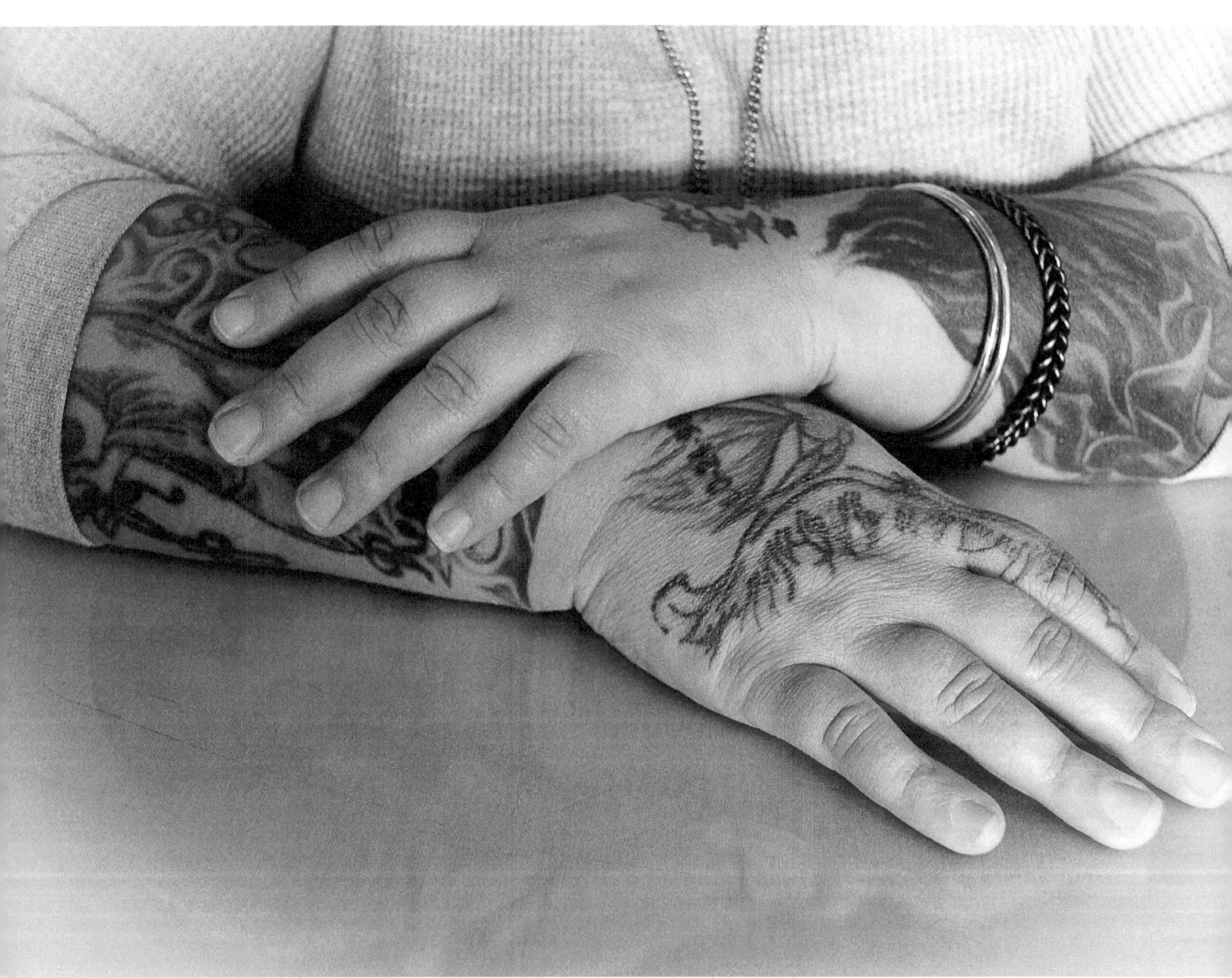

Of The Hands
　　　Shamecca Long

Heartache has a way of showing in hands:
calloused pain from dragging yesterday's load.
Some days I search for softness in her face,
a face I try to make home.

Try to make room
Try to make mother

Her body is foreign
My mouth filled with silence
Cluttered childhood
The blood of curiosity
Fucking audacity!
Blotches of hues ensue
after long nights of booze
I still pull myself
inside out
Could never grasp
what was found in empty bottles.

Now I know:
　　　you wasn't looking,
　　　　　you was running
from hands loud with stories
fingers full of memories
of each heart drop
each heart race
ears zoned into intruding doors.

Nails rich with DNA
Shame hiding in lining of dresses.

These hands hold you accountable
for warm beds and quiet
For grown men and hymen
These hands know battle
These hands know defeat
These hands know cruelty
but they also know redemption.
These hands are raising a daughter
who's both innocence and balled fists.
Guerrera and princess,
we are scorched earth and rebirth.

These hands learn forgiveness
These hands learn living
These hands learn…

I can continue hating you
but it will only kill me
and we are too grand for dying.
These hands let go
These hands know
you will always be familiar betrayal.

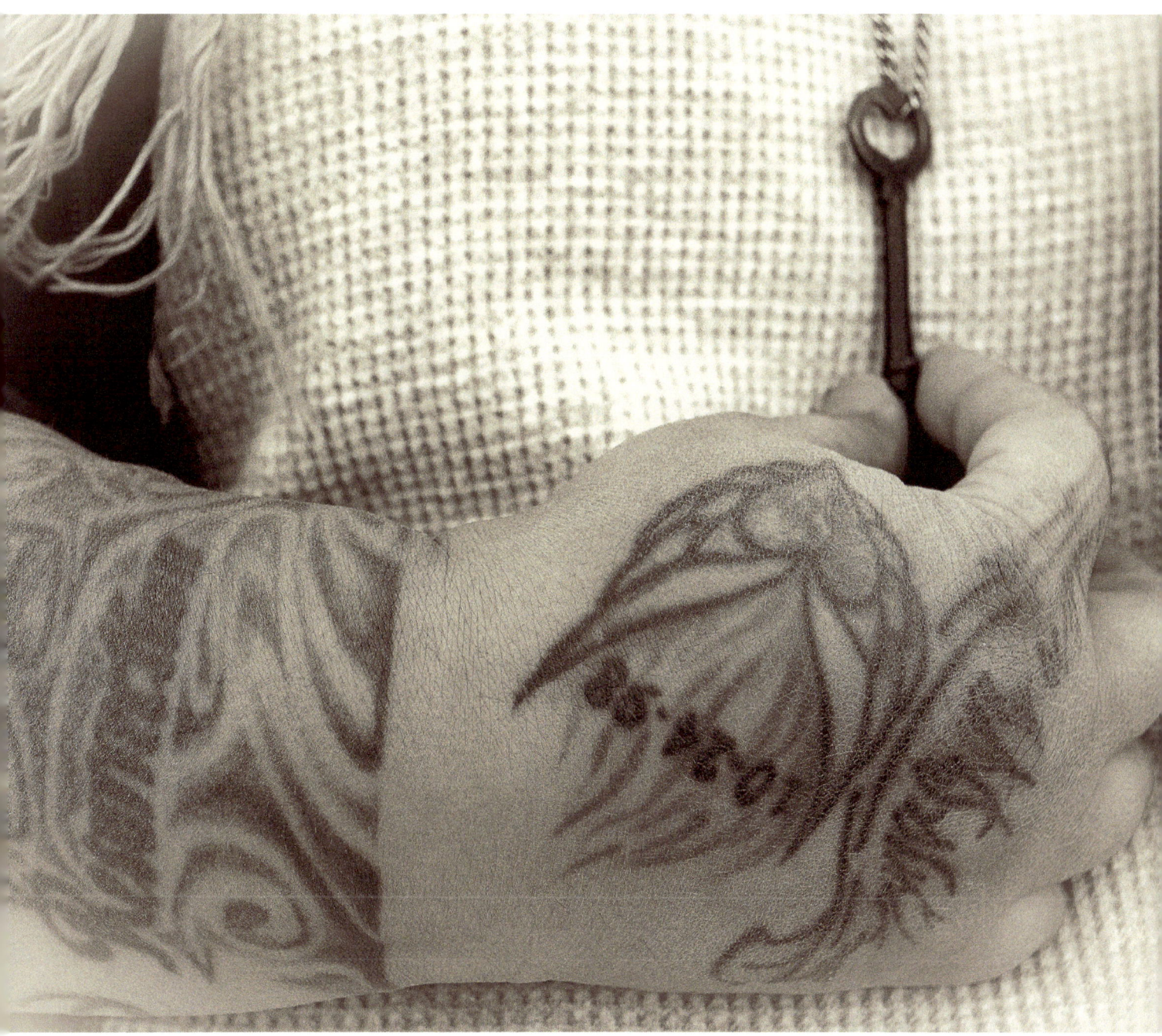

Anoche viendo vídeo de La Yiyiyi en YouTú con la abuela que nunca llegué a conocer
or La Lupe's Voice is a Full-Bodied Feeling
         <u>Annette Estévez</u>

                                                                  El consuelo abraza con delirio,
                                                                        fatiga, obsesión de gloria.

                                                       Deseo: el diablo cuerpo sin fin
                                                           tengo dentro de mí
                                                    igual en un dolor necesario.

                     Que bien queda.
                     Es forma de ser
                     destrozar mi corazón
                     que llora
                     ¡soy la mala! bien ensayada.

                                                     Destrozar mi corazón
                                                   que llora, que crea,
                                                       parece que
                                                           perdona.

                Te pedí que supieras vida
                amor que pudiera en tus manos poner
                la luz para ti,

                      ser
                      las estrellas,
                      el sol,
                      un Dios,
                      así como amor,   más.

To My Grandmother's Shadow
　　　　Nia Andino

I write to you at the foot of trees because they
sway sturdy in their glorious decay. I wish you
could leave your darkness here. Bathe in the light
of sundial limbs and rest your fight. My songs
have character because of you. I just wish I could
slumber your afflictions with them. I am forever
searching. But when I find the right song,
I will sing it for you.

　　　Forever,
　　　Your Little White Bird

Manos de La Doña
> Bernice Sosa

La Doña's hands clutched her Bible all the way to her coffin. Shrills of agony trapped within palm creases, upon the book she'd claim saved her spirit before Alzheimer's met her acquaintance. I watched tears somersault toward jawline, unlike those shed at his father's departure. That day he clutched thornless white rose, caressed petals between soft whimpers as holy waterfalls cleansed tortured spirit. That day white blooms rained upon El Don's casket, gently kissing cannon fist, verbal dart nightmares goodnight.

Papi's monosyllabic utterances of La Doña filled empty seats,
left in espera, at the Ortiz Funeral Home.

> "That's mom."
> "Poor mom."
> "Pop used to beat her."
> "You look just like her."
> "You look like mom."

Papi's mom. La Doña, whose perfect posture never bent.
Stiff nerved vertebrae, head propped high,
eyes recording blows and objects hurled by the man who cried love.

La Doña, whose malevolent laughter blanketed daughters' pleas for predator salvation and smothered sons' sobbing hearts mute. La Doña who passed down amargura y dolor from first born to last, dangled spirits over damnation – head down, ankles up –'til the lights went out.

La Doña. The one I should call Abuela. Owner of hands I cannot recall around my shoulders in embrace; whose fingers I cannot recall caressing my frizzy locks in cariño; whose prints left their last mark on the cover of a book of a God she claimed to praise:

"Alabaré, alabaré, alabaré, alabaré, alabaré a mi Señor…"

Alabaré – she would praise her señor until he beat her and their children senseless, time and time again. Until the seven were plucked from her absent grip, terrified babies distributed amongst foreign residences. The empty seats of Ortiz Funeral were filled with tortured ghosts whose vessels chose not to attend, and sat adjacent to abandoned souls present for La Doña's despedida.

This day there were no white roses, whimpers or heavy tears. Just even tones slipping through the vocal chords of La Doña's black sheep, solemn and sober. As his daughter, her only grandchild of bearing resemblance, air-kissed future reflection through closed lids, heart anesthetized, by inherited abandon.

The Resignation Letter
        <u>Rebeca Lois Lucret</u>

You want me to call you by name
A name perhaps given through incantation or magic
A name perhaps given through ceremony or ritual
A name perhaps given after a spirit animal
Perhaps passed down the tribal totem
Gifted by elders traveled over sand and seas
Perhaps it was that epic
Perhaps it was as simple as sound
A name told- you dressed in honor
A name told -you demanded respect
A name told- you rooted in rights
But not today
Not on this very last day
Not while the sun dances to the joy in my chest
Not while I address you as
To Whom It May Concern
To a certain no one in particular
To anyone simply because it just doesn't matter
I am leaving

Today I chant me a vision of a life once put on hold
I am an Indian dance in a blessing of rain
Already I feel the harvest prospering behind breastbone
Today let us be mindful in the hours to come
Let us remember all you've stolen from us, from me
Let me declare on this day of pirate's treasure
The wealth of becoming whole again
Of walking among the world, rightfully intact
Let us be present in the hours that remain
Let us know that the maiming of your name is forever

To whom it may concern:
Today I break bread with love

Today during the final hour
A sunrise promises colors
A garden will grow out of the welts you've left
Hummingbirds will sing a song of freedom
A gate will appear around the foliage
You are not allowed in
I don't care whose name you carry
I am leaving

Today I speak only my name
Honor my name
Respect my name
Have its melody put the grandbabies to sleep
Have its warmth fill a home left for winters
Have its life revive a culture of home

I once forgot I, too, had a name
I once forgot I, too, held power
I am leaving

Yours truly,

Abuela sabe renacer

IV

Two Moons: *'tu:, 'mu:ns* Doreen Asia Headen Synonym- Gamma

1. Bronx beadworker, spiritualist and cathartic writer who descends from the Chickasaw and Cherokee Nations. 2. Born on a solar eclipse; fearless woman of resolved grit; see lightworker. 3. Nine is a significant number: siblings, grandchildren, birthday month and day, traced her family line starting in 1999. 4. Spirit animals: dolphin and wolf for security and freedom to live in any of the cardinal directions. 5. Embraced her history later in life and was reborn from troubled child to Spofford alumni to Soundview spiritualist: see the importance of knowing roots; finding foundation; maiz pushing up on concrete. 6. Believes in the power of purpose, faith and legacy; see four corners song and dance. 7. Revivir.

Last Rites Haiku
> Peggy Robles Alvarado

Thirsty and gasping,
she called for God and Mamá-
They're one and the same

Coatlicue

    Katalina Rodriguez

You are Coatlicue
Aztec Earth Mother Goddess
vessel of the duality of woman,
creator and destroyer

You are woman mother sister daughter
guided by a lineage of guerreras curanderas y brujas
Your path rooted in the wisdom of Atzlan
runs so deep even the earth's soil
knows you by name

You are mi Abuelita
deep almond eyes
hands coco brown
skin rich and soft
like silk woven with the finest threads
Each line and wrinkle holds secrets
mysteries of generations of Ortega women

Your hands
patting and kneading blue corn tortillas
like our Bisabuelas once did
looking out from pyramid walls

Your sorceress-like hands
creating the intoxicating aroma of fresh cooked maiz
that dances with the thick Michuacan air
filled with the scent of avocado trees
and the mysteries held in the cerros y montañas

I inhale this mixture
immediately my body and spirit recognize
they are home

Your long thick salt and pepper hair
cascades past your small frame
It carries a life of its own
one not limited by the years of your body

Memories of me as a little girl braiding your hair
while sitting on your lap
floods my psyche
Even then I knew you were magical
Your essence glowed
I was forever branded by our moments
though few

You are Coatlicue
Aztec   Earth   Mother   Goddess
The essence of womanhood
A reflection of all Ortega women
An embodiment of our lineage
My muse
My Abuelita
Me

Headaches and Heartaches

    Karina Guardiola-Lopez

Mi abuelita soaked wet leaves in a small towel
It smelled like soil, sand and the sea
A combination of all and in between
    She said it was:
    ruda con yerbabuena
    agua florida y alcoholado
    All contained tightly inside a can
She then recited:
A prayer   A proverb   A psalm
    She gently pressed her petite palms
    on my forehead
    My pain was hers too
    "Pobrecita mi niña"
When my eyes were closed
I spoke to G-d
Prayed to remove the
Bricks and sticks
stones and boulders
    I was only 5 when the migraines began
    It was hard to do homework
    I remained strong and held in my tears
    while inhaling the scent of mint, earth and rain
    a combination hard to explain
I still try this now at home
When the NSAIDs fail to work
I know that G-d is the healer
but I know he used my Abuelita's touch
because she was a devoted kneeler
and still a believer

She Shifted the Weight
   Claudia Whittingham

She pushed the weight of her grandmother's tongue
from her mouth making way for foreign teeth,
ripping the truth away from her own beauty.
He reminded her: "I gave you a rib,
what'chu gonna give me?"

Her feet never cradled the earth. Sharp grains of sand
never harbored between her toes. Red clay never soothed
the trials of her life. "There are no flowers here", he said
as he reminded her: "I gave you a rib,
what'chu gonna give me?"

She spit out her grandmother's tongues; Ashanti lullabies
morphed into jazz beats adrift in the ocean near the bones
of those craving the comfort of Yemaya's palace.
Shifting into Olokun's domain, salty waters exploding over
chains, obliterating flesh and all the lies their ancestors told
themselves in languages foreign to their souls because
they had to survive.

She spit out her grandmother's tongues in my mouth.
Those tongues took root in rhythms and melodies
flowing between a rib carved into my teeth and planted
flowers that have never been trampled by feet.

Between Birds and Shadows
   Nia Andino

Dear White Bird,
Today feels like sable, but I am used to it raining black pepper. Boring holes and burn marks into memories, that leave constant reminders of who I am not, in eyes that look like mine. I put sick on your tongue more than I care to. Question why my thoughts are scavengers for scars or why I tend to the cries of strangers in my head before yours? I wander between worlds that don't merge and tainted soil. One moment, I am loving you. The next, I am stocking chambers for sorrow in your chest when I want to say the things that grandmothers do - those caring things, those tender things of fragrant birds.

I want to speak to you in only one language instead of our light walking on earthquakes. Praying that this day will be solid. And still, I want to stop feeding you hope from old soup tureens, push down cotton ball levees to quell the screeching. The screeching that echoes for days after it has left my rabid throat when I jumble your image with ghosts that beg. I want to measure you in the creases of hugs left along my side. My tired cactus side. Burn the thorns with my envy of you in palo santo when you speak of dream things and your luxury of youth is loved heavy for it. If I could suffocate the seasons of madness for more days that won't change the corners of your lips into low swinging arcs, I would.

I think of ways to leave you a legacy beyond carrying apple sack bones. I think of ways to raise my tenderness like a slow boil of beans, and I think of ways of how to untwist this guilt knotted around my neck. Each morning, I await the bloom of a vegetated quiet from ingesting shiny ovals and anticipate dry docks under your eyes. But most of all, I pray that you don't inherit these parts of me. And I pray, that you never curse the blessed moon for my lunacies.

Love,
Grandmother Moon

About "Abuela"
> Vanessa "Nessa" Acevedo

Abuela: Niña/ Mujer/ Hermana/ Sobrina/ Tía
Prima/ Amiga/ Novia/ Suegra/ Esposa
Cuñada/ Madre/ Viajera
Organismo complejo

*   If you mark the date your own Mami gave birth to you as the beginning of Nona's identity, you're really missing out. The term "Abuela" is just a dot on the timeline between you and your Mami. Abuela is a woman with a history, an impact, a portal to a way.

**   Yes, your technology confuses her. She doesn't understand your need to compute the freshness from the Earth. When you really listen, you'll understand that the bright screen does not warm like backwoods fed hearth.

***   If you pace your mind through the rough terrain of her life of squalor you will be sure to appreciate the smoothed packed earth beneath your feet. You will worry less about grass stains from tall blades slick with 19th century tears and sweat, as the dew of blessed days will be extracted from the twilight of oppression.

****   Abuela might mark the date your Mami gave birth to you as a new chance to show that her suffering was not in vain. So, if in her attempt to explain to you she cuts her wrist, attempts to prove herself human, don't panic. Wrap her up in love and respect. Show her how your Mami taught you blame is useless.

What Abuela Carries
Alexandra Hernandez

Abuela carries a large wooden spoon
to stir the pot of hearty sopa
we use for healing
for a cold, a bad day,
for a broken heart - especially then;
it is our medicine.

She carries the pain of it,
our heartache.
She may not always understand it, or agree.
But she pushes against the weight of it,
our defeat.

Abuela carries our brown eyes,
our Taino tanned skin, our dark hair,
although hers has long gone gray.
She passes them on
and on down the line
and as we grow, we cut it, we dye it
we change.
But she carries our original form,
for it was hers to begin with.

Abuela carries his heart in hers.
She keeps it there,
like a secret.
Their secret.
Maybe she knew from the beginning,
that he wouldn't always be hers.
Before her, he belonged to another.

Nights spent dancing in
corners of darkened rooms,
surrounded by strangers
that could never judge them.
Those memories-
she carries them too.

Abuela carries that baby in her belly,
That baby she didn't plan.
That baby is my mother.

She is heavy.
Heavy with love she already has
for a child she has never met.
She is already her pride and joy.
With this blessing, she also carries
guilt, anger, pain.

Most of all,
Abuela carries strength.
She carries hope.
She holds it high for us to see
when she wipes away our tears,
when she feeds our bellies.
Abuela carries proof
that even in darkness,
there is light.

Abuela sabe sanar

V

Maggie Castro Stevens: *mægɪ, KAS-tro, steevns* Synonym - Grandma

1. Self- healing faithful woman who understands the stretch can help prevent the break; see ujjayi method; wave breathing and lotus position. 2. Recognizes what and who matters by looking in the eyes of her grandson. 3. Opened el cielo in her throat with a freestyle song. 4. Surrendered to resting pose and Sankofa and rebranded her vulnerabilities as gifts. 5. Crafted an archetype for an Abuela when her only model was a toothy snarl and a regaño. 6. Released the pesadumbre that darkened under the eyes and in the chest in exchange for folding her arms around the ones she chooses to hold; see Wild Thing Pose/ Camatkarasana. 7. Restaurada.

What Abuela Carried
Vanessa "Chica" Ferreira

Abuela carried the weight
of her country, silently,
while Abuelo worked
Trujillo's fields.
He reminded her that he
gave her that rib.
She tended to the boys and
one girl, the "wild" one
whom she attempted
to tame with broomsticks
and tight braids.
Abuela let go
of her country once
she arrived to
the United States.
Unwilling to return,
not even for a visit,
while Abuelo made
frequent trips,
making children
without her.

This Poem is an Unfinished Hanging Thing
Annette Estévez

> We have that in common.
> The last thing my therapist told me
> was to see a psychiatrist.
>
> I haven't
> visited my grandmother's grave.
>
> It's somewhere outside my window.
> We have only met in gloom.
>
> My mother searches for her mother
> and finds me.
>
> I have many
> pieces. I know something's mine
> if it's broken.
>
> Some days I can feel something shift.
>
> There is someone
> slicing an orange in my head.
> Each slice is a jellyfish.
>
> They do not sting. They stick. They feed.
>
> My grandmother poured the kitchen down my
> grandfather's throat as he slept.

My mother searches
for her mother's depression
and finds me.

My grandmother rests somewhere
outside my window.

We have only met in womb -

my mother

is four years old,
peering into a psych ward

my bedroom door swings open.

Dos Abuelas
> Karina Guardiola-Lopez

I have two Abuelitas
perhaps just like you
One who raised me
and one I never knew

One raised Catholic
One raised Baptist
One named Tabora
One named Sandoval
One married a Connor
One married a Guardiola

One real close,
a very shapely
seamstress
One so far, only met her
in photos and stories

Both Honduran
with blood from Spain
with similar history
running through
their veins

Both with a granddaughter
curious about her history

One DNA identified
One remains a mystery

We're Still Dying
    Rebeca Lois Lucret

    She was smaller after every episode.
    The hour had come again when we'd
    need to empty the contents. Another
    round of removing more, as if breast
    wasn't enough.

    I dumped the brown jellies, the red and the pink,
    the sometimes mucus and thinning
    liquid into the toilet. She always watched it settle
    before I flushed, before I repositioned the tube and
    checked the incision for colors of danger.

        I remember taking her hands in mine,
        guiding them under the faucet so she'd
        wash her hands, but she always grew numb.
        No movement. No comment. No questions.
        Only silence and the running faucet.

        Silence and shrinkage.
        Silence and defeat.
        Silence and death.

        Preying vultures aim.
            Both raven and crow circle
                the heads of women.

Infarto: a zuihitsu set to bolero
Peggy Robles- Alvarado

Dios te salve Maria, llena eres de gracia, el señor esté contigo

> The truth is, women are less likely to call 9-1-1 when experiencing symptoms of a heart attack themselves. It simply doesn't occur to them to do so. The bulk of media attention on the disease is focused on men.
>
> -goredforwomen.org

You are an excited and confused 6,
rushed out of school before the math test,
your open Barbie book bag: a wailing mouth
sputtering homework onto the sidewalk
as you run to Tía Lucia's apartment.
Mami's eyes are pomegranate, speckled
and bulging. At the door you are clutched in
rosary beads, recitation, and last rites
released from the clenched teeth of 7 of her
16 now motherless children kneeling around
Tía's Spanish style floral sofá, where Mamá
Lolita, in a blue dress as if ready for the sky,
has gone to meet the God she talked to so often.

> "Papá era un bruto. Put his prints all over her Sunday best.
> Reminded her often that he gave her that rib."
> – Mami talking to herself in a dark kitchen
> after too many beers and boleros

Bendita tú eres entre todas las mujeres, Bendito sea el fruto de tu vientre Jesús

BLAMMMMM BLAM bang bang BLAMMMMMmmmm
                      HOOOOOOOOOooooooooooooh
Everything you got/ girl/is mine
BLAM BLAM   ya undastand
Sit down 'n shut up
        -Ntozake Shange, Expiriese Girl Wanted

In the United States, 1 in 4 women dies from heart disease.
Heart diseases that affect women more than men include:
- Coronary microvascular disease- (MVD) a problem that affects the heart's tiny arteries
- Broken heart syndrome - extreme emotional stress leading to severe but often short-term heart muscle failure

    -U.S. National Library of Medicine

You are a wandering and curious 22 searching
for the heart of stories ready for telling. Tape
recorder pulsing, you dissect Mami hoping to
find Abuela, pushing on the silence, gnawing
at sinew, willing to break bones for the marrow of
her. Mami's eyes are Olokun's graveyard:
shadowy keeper of the dead's secrets. You push.
Examine her chest for rise and fall then suddenly
she bursts: fists over ribcage, the motherless child
gasps for air. Memory threatens to smoother
arteries. Pressure rising, she sputters:
    "She was too weak to leave him and
    I couldn't protect her anymore."

Santa Maria, Madre de Dios, ruega por ella y por nosotros pecadores,
ahora y en la hora de nuestra muerte, Amén

> That was enough
> for me to forgive you.
> To spirit a tiger
> from its cell.
> -Sandra Cisneros,
> You called Me Corazón

After the Heartbreak
    Shamecca Long
  (To my daughter)

Locked behind what seems to be opportunity,
having interviewed for role of past girlfriend,
drowning in new heartbreak,
trying to be better lifeguard-

I hear you
wishing yourself water.
More life, more force
to a dam of a boyfriend.
It's over
but you are not finished.

Learn how to float with life
pummeling your back.
You won't sink.
Don't think heartbreak
equals earthquake.

Your world is not split in two
it has simply removed a leech.
Please understand, there's no need for
hand me down love.

It leaves you starved, brittle, bitter
feeding on yourself.
And we know hunger intimately.

Your grandmother, in a twenty year
marriage, experienced famine.
Her mouth harvesting blades,
A love so barren managed to raise
five children, bury two.

Continue through suffering.
Don't be fooled, a brick house
is still hollow.

Resist carbon copy.

Never remove magic from your bones
for a man versed in ~~disappearing~~ acts.

Remember how water can be cleansing.
Your water is renewing.

These are the fruits mothers yield.

Abuela sabe moverse

VI

Addie Diaz- Siverio: *ad-ee, dee-ahs, si-veh-ree-o* Synonym: Nani

1. Timeless, opulent woman of beauty and skill. 2. Mujer of muscle and movement. 3. Teaches the body's joy in eight step counts throughout Japan, London, Switzerland, San Francisco, Westchester and the boogie down Bronx; see Addie-Tude Dance Company. 4. Prowess en cada paso emblazoned with beads, glitter or lace. 5. Has suffered from Latin madness since a very young age; hysteria of the hips a la Millie Donay, Rita Moreno and Debbie Allen. 6. Built her legacy with sequin and styling on 2; see Mambo, Descarga Latina and Salsa Congress. 7. Dichosa.

Rebound Haiku
Shamecca Long

Brushes foundation
Across the latest heartbreak
It is ladies night

In Leticia's Kitchen Drawer
    <u>Peggy Robles Alvarado</u>

        A Craftsman curved claw hammer to crack coco and hang portraits, a tape measure to remind her waist she eats mangú too often, fifteen scattered rusty pennies to help Tito with math homework or sink into a nine day candle to cut Doña Elsa's evil eye on any given day, five slightly bent nails pulled from the living room wall that held portraits proving they danced merengue once, a red silk ribbon to tie his picture to her sweaty discount store underwear to keep him from falling back into Tanya's bed, wrinkled menus from the Goodie- Goodie Thai restaurant on Cruger she treats herself to when her sister mocks her for never getting a passport or mispronouncing Pinot Noir, or not having any Sears family portraits, a ball of white yarn to wrap around pasteles every Christmas or to secure lucky leaves above the doorway when he drinks both their paychecks, film from an outdated Kodak she won't develop to avoid seeing the exact day she lost her looks on his knuckles, ginger candy from the Korean market she reluctantly pushes in her mouth every time he dares her to leave, every time her tongue lashes a familiar whip to her body, and when her voice mimics her sister's burn, Diamond long stick matches for lighting the broken pilot light and the candles that keep her bowing to him.

¡Basta!
    <u>Maria Rivas</u>

"Mother, please don't die without sinning."

"What? "

"Yeah, mom there's a halo on your head."

"I got married at 13. I didn't have time to sin."

"But wasn't there a want or need to commit at least one major sin?"

"No, mija"

"Pero, 42 years with the same man is a long time and you're a hot mom."

"Oh, niña you're the only one who asks these questions."

"Can you at least invent something? Humor me. Lie to me. I just want to believe your flesh desired and lived life."

"I did live life. What do you think this is?"

"What, the Mercedes and the houses?"

"¡Sí! Esta es la vida."

"That doesn't mean you lived life, it just means you paid for it. What does a Mercedes or a house do for your soul?"

"¿Cuál soul mija? I was hungry and now I 'm not."

"But…"

"No buts, ni que buts. When you realize that generations of your family were born and died barefoot, it's survival"

"You sold your soul?"

"Daydreaming about a soul is an American luxury. No, I just cashed in. I said - Hasta aquí llegó el hambre. No mujer alegre for me. I will not be paid to make men happy. I'm going to be rich."

"Mujer alegre?"

"Sí, a prosti. Not me."

"So, you married for money?"

"No, it was an investment. My dream was to be a businesswoman."

"That's the same thing."

"You have too much free time. I own this empire- I built it."

"With my father's money."

"No, with my sudor y lágrimas."

"Mother that sounds like…"

"Like what? A sinner? A prostitute? Like what? Esta vida no es pa' pendejas."

"Pero, mother."

"I was poor and illiterate but I wasn't stupid. There's a difference."

"He didn't care that you came from a family of …?"

"What? Of putas? Mija please, his family had a long line of those too. Money either hides or erases everything- the past or the present."

"Pero, you always say, "lo que se hace de noche, de día aparece."

"True. But if you know who to hire then all can be hidden or erased."

"Is that why we don't know anyone from your side of the family?"

"Mija, are you hungry?"

"No."

"Are you barefoot?"

"No."

"Are you a prosti?"

"No."

"Then there's nothing more for you to ask. If you want to invent or recreate my past, or my present fill it up with sins but don't ever question why I did it. I was going to be rich y basta."

A Timeline
    Vanessa "Nessa" Acevedo

When was the first time
anger found rhythm in a pounding heart?
Judgment- a throne at the peak of ego?
Punishment- a place in a mutilated mind?
Control- a grip in a knotted fist?

What were the first syllables to come together
and solidify concepts like:

bitch, whore, slut
piece of shit, good for nothing
damaged
cualquiera

Why did anyone prefer
a role for a gender, an age?
A place for a race, a class?
A definition for a right and a wrong?
An agreement of a crime and a
meting out of a punishment?

Who was the first to agree?
the second to support?
the third to proclaim?
the fourth to affirm?
the fifth to legislate?
the sixth to execute?

Oh, it snowballed even through the desert!
Continues to roll well into 63 years after
mi Abuela was cast out of her home for having
the nerve to get pregnant with a life of her own.
63 years and 10 months after she abandoned the
notion that her life could be more than what
society saw in her uterine bundle.

And so my Mami was left
shallowly planted in salted earth.
Left to fend for herself against the pesticides of
sexism and patriarchy. Sprayed with harsh
chemical words and body parts seeking to poison her.
Preserve her for the sake of eating her alive.
The chewing toughened her enough to
become inedible to man.
Nurturing only to her own seeds,
to those wise enough to notice thorns
and be pleased with inhaling her aroma.

I was fortunate to sprout nutritious to need,
poisonous to ignorance, especially my own.
God only knows what hearty version of all this
my own children will be birthed to.
God, I am certain, they will travel their journeys
with the grace of a viajera.
Expert map readers,
suited for blazing trails of their own, and
well versed in syllabic utterances of love.

Bonita
(A Monologue to her Unborn Daughter)
<u>Alexandra Hernandez</u>

What am I going to do? Dios mio. What am I going to do? A baby. A child. Am I really that dumb? How could I have been so stupid to think that I am so special that I could do anything I wanted with no repercussions? That I could give myself over to someone who is practically a stranger, a married man at that! And what? No price to pay for the innocent, little Bonita? The pretty one, the fun one, the can't-do-no-wrong one? What a joke, Bonnie. Everything you thought - Wrong. Wrong.

No wonder your family is abandoning you Bonita, little by little. You boasted about moving to New York and being some kind of success, better than the others. But you've messed up! You didn't think it through. You used your heart instead of your mind. You used your body instead of your brain. Carajo Bonita! Did your mother teach you nothing? You ask yourself all of these questions now. Now that you're pregnant and half loca.

The point is, loca or not, this is happening. No turning back now. Are you showing up anytime soon, little one? 'Cause we gotta get out of here. I think I might need you more than I realize. The more I think about it, you're my sidekick now, my little confidante. It's just me and you in the big, bad world. Me and you, forever. I'm scared, you know? I'm scared about what it's gonna be like when you're out here and we're out there. I pray and pray every night that we'll be okay. I can't make any promises but I can pray.

My dear daughter, mi hija, I'm doing what I can to keep it together but you should know, before you make your grand entrance, that I've made some mistakes. Big ones. Listen up! I know you can hear me so let me just get this out now because when you're here, it's all going to change for me. You're about to turn my life upside down. And I know you didn't ask for this! No, this is all me. But we've got to be a team. I'm going to take care of us. We'll take care of each other.

I can see you now. Long, pelo negro. Big, beautiful eyes. Maybe like your father's. And every time I look into them, I'll think of him fondly and without hate. You'll have your mama's wide, curvy hips and love of cooking. Together, we'll make pasteles, arroz, flan y coquito. We'll be queens, you and I!

But the most important thing I'm going to tell you is this- You will not be like me. You might have my little nose, my puffy lips, my giant forehead, but you'll be smarter than me. I'll make sure of that. You'll do big things, hija. You'll see the whole damn world. Not like me, not like me. This life isn't for you. I'll love you with my heart and soul, mamita. I already do. But we won't be going through this a second time.

You'll be a giant. And you'll be my daughter. And you'll be better than us all…

Consejos That Remind Me I Am Her (Grand) Daughter
Peggy Robles- Alvarado

Always wash your panties by hand
Never put your cartera on the floor
Don't cut your hair while on your period

En noche buena, burn incense right before midnight
Feed the birds left over bread, they're God's messengers
Put a glass of water under your bed to prevent nightmares

        Wear red lipstick to drown out the dark circles under your eyes
        Don't stand in front of an open freezer after you get out of the shower
        Soak cebolla in honey for three days, take a spoonful para la congestión

Blend garlic, pimiento verde y cilantro for a stockpile of sofrito, keep it in the fridge
Stash small bundles of cash tied with a red ribbon in all the plaster cast saints
When you have a cold put Vick's on the soles of your feet and cover them with socks

Collect snow from the first winter storm and
mop your floors with it, eso es agua bendita

Put a glass of water by the front door
to absorb negative energy
and bochinche from vecinos

Always talk to water, it holds memoria,
escucha, it's a mouthpiece
to God

Abuela sabe luchar

VII

Shihan Candy Warixi Soto
Shee-han, kan-dee, wah-rik-shee, so-to Synonym - Bibi

1. Strong, steadfast, espiritista and champion who channels éxito; see Bushido ring, and rank of Kaiden in Miyama Ryu Combat Ju-Jitsu. 2. Disciplined when breaking barriers and making her - story history; see grandmaster, martial arts hall of fame, woman of the year, and organizations she founded: female alternative street tactics and secure your child. 3. Understands the balance between war and peace, ashes and incense, street fighting and kata. 4. As guardian of her Bohío, she donated her kidney to her guaili and gave him a second life after the womb. 5. Defying notions of extinction, she calls on Taíno resurrection and rewrites caciques and jíbaros into poetry, art and song; see founder of Taíno Awards and head of the Tanama Tribe. 6. Whisperer of weeping willows in Pelham Bay Park who calls on the wind with a maraca, a crown of brown feathers and a katana strapped to her side. 7. Persistir.

Aquella Abuela
　　　Shihan Candy Warixi Soto

　　　　　　　　　　　Aquella Abuela indiecita, la que nunca conocí,
　　　　　　　　　　　　　　las Abuelas de mis Bisabuelas,
　　　　　　aquellas que sufrieron en las manos de los invasores.
　　　　　Las que no tuvieron remedio. Las que se quedaron solas.
　　　　　　　　Las que tuvieron que enseñar a sus hijos
　　　　　　　　　las tradiciones, ceremonias y canciones.

Canciones ya calladas con el tiempo.
Canciones a las siete direcciones,
a la tierra, a las aguas, al sol y la luna.

　　　　　　　　　　　　Aquella Abuelita que nunca conocí.
　　　　　　　　　　La que oró por mí, su futura generación.
　　　　　La que lloró como oro y lloro yo ahora, para el futuro.

Aquella Abuelita con sus manos hecha callo de tanto trabajo.
Aquella que fue madre, guerrera, y curandera.
Que aun con miedo al invasor se atrevió a mantener,
en secreto, sus creencias y tradición.

　　　　　Aquella Abuelita
　　　　　　Aquella Abuelita
　　　　　　　Aquella Abuelita

　　　　　Sangre de mi sangre, tenía valor,
　　　y aunque no la conocí, la llevo en mis venas.
　　　　　Ahí es que viven todas mis Abuelas.

Memorandum of understanding
between a granddaughter
and the sabelo-todos
    Peggy Robles- Alvarado

The night you died it rained sapphire daggers from the midnight sky over the mountains in Jaguas. They cut into the rooftop of the one room casita Papá had built for you and your ten hungry children. The darkness above competing with the darkness below. Each raindrop slicing into what was left of your skin on bone. A tormenta to couple the one you cursed up each time death sent one of its messengers; a chirping grillo stacking nine rows of pebbles by the doorway, or a guaraguao with a kola nut in its beak perched on a rotten tree stump by the latrine. That night the messengers sent to ease your burning ovaries were met with howling wind that danced the blue blades and turbulent deluge deeper into your flesh.

Your mouth opened, not for a final breathe but for a drink, for this was holy water of wind and thunder. You parted your lips, uncurled your tongue, coaxed at the lightening trapped in your throat, prompting a final moan that shattered the window panes.

This was not the death they envisioned. Not the one each of your girls prayed up for you. There were no archangels and easy rolling back of the eyes because you were of night people. You were of jaguars with one eye that only appeared when the moon eclipsed over El Rio Cialitos. You were of humans born with wings deemed demons and cast out by the neighbors saved by mission pastors. Their crosses never burned you but their doctors did; pulled your bile, your blue- black blood and mistook it for illness.

Gente del monte don't bleed the same. Their marrow is thicker, the blood rushes opposite from the heart, pulls from all directions, a current all its own that challenges rivers and oceans. There are no scientific journals to define your people; the opener of roads, los perros de palo, that find paths en carreteras no marcadas. Usted es de mujeres raras con afecto pequeño y rastros agresivos.

Those cerulean blades, the relentless torrent of celestial waves, cut into you not out of hate or anger. The sky and valley had opened all at once, releasing its ocean just to carry you home. The moon witnessed the blue- black veins of the night sky dull the stars at half- staff to soothe you, piece by piece. They were all spectators in your leaving, in the departing of a misunderstood, only one, mujer única, en un barrio de sabelo-todos, where your mouth was a most feared weapon they had no idea how to praise.

I Was Supposed to Be My Grandmother's Namesake
or
A Crown of Twelve Stars
      Annette Estévez

I wanna know what made your bones rattle.
I could ask them.

Would it require a prayer I don't believe in?
What did you pray for?

I'm running out of ways to run away
from myself.

Alone in a museum where your name
adorns every wall,
I learn Guadalupe means
hidden river.

I write this down in Spanish for you to read.

La Virgen laughs, covering
her mouth with her hand,
swings a machete over the "i".

Abuela and í (become) escape.

108

The Treatment
    PaulA Neves

> *You remembered huge events which had quite probably not happened, you remembered the details of incidents without being able to recapture their atmosphere, and there were long blank periods to which you could assign nothing. Everything had been different then. Even the names of countries, and their shapes on the map, had been different.*
>
> --George Orwell, 1984

You went out with her almost every day that summer for her pick-ups—only the good stuff, the best weed. Feverfew. Dandelion. Lemongrass. Violet. You name it, she knew it. Or, she named it and she knew it. To this day you can only guess what she picked from the swaths surrounding Newark's sidewalks and Mosquito Park paths to make her stew. That's right, her stew. And you were the main ingredient.

1973. You didn't have much meat on you but you were already tall for your age, which wasn't exactly an accomplishment. The Portuguese are little. When you blurted one Sunday morning, as your mother watered the front stoop marigolds before church, that Senhoras Maria Conceição and Maria Isaura, the old crabs who lived across the street and told you to get off their driveway when your ball rolled in it, looked like the flying monkeys on the Wizard of Oz, Ma popped you so hard on the mouth the wad of Bazooka Joe you pinched from the closet Halloween stash flew out of your mouth and earned you another whack. "No, no, no," you scrambled for the right word. "I meant…midgets." Whack! For the next hour your face throbbed in the pew at Our Lady of Fatima, aka Wizard's Palace.

It was these tendencies that made you firmly believe you didn't need Graciete. You were already too grown to need her. And now, as you're often told by those who have more important things to think about, no one else needs to hear about her, or any of them either. But you are not so sure.

So there she was in the flesh, in your house. Graciete. Not Maria like your Ma, aunts, cousins, the midgets, and every Latin mother of Jesus, no matter what her sins. Just for the record, though, you weren't a Maria either. Didn't even get a middle name. "It sounds more American," Ma explained when you worried something was missing. You were a little Freudian even then.

"But Miguel has a middle name, and so do you and Pai."

"Never mind." She waved you off and went back to boiling diapers, or Ballpark Franks.

And now here was another relative. Did she have more than one name? You didn't have time to ask.

"Avé Maria! This child needs treatment!" Graciete exploded by way of hello.

You were standing in that linoleum Newark kitchen—you, your mother, and now her mother, Graciete. Graciete, your grandmother, who bent down, grasped your arms and turned them over, shaking her head at the scabs and crusts. You tried to pull away, but she added, "And on the legs too!"

Chickenpox. An incurable strain. Incurable as in Ma and Pai had no money to buy another lotion from the farmácia. Incurable as in forget about taking time off from work to take you to the clínica.

Ma peeled carrots and potatoes for a cosido at the sink. Pai sat drinking his more-wine-than-soda spritzers in the living room. Walter Cronkite droned on the black and white Zenith about the latest POW. Pai was already on his third spritzer just ten minutes after arriving with Graciete from the airport.

You know what they're going to expect you to type next:

The house was one of those railroad types - four rooms, each one opening into the other.

Well, it was. And two-year-old Miguel lay napping in your shared "car," the bed-crammed vestibule between the kitchen and the living room. We make our own myths.

Pai cleared his throat and shifted on the creaky armchair. That chair and the equally clamorous couch had already hosted cousins from Rhode Island, Canada, Venezuela - places as far away from Lafayette St. as the Portugal they'd left. But you knew Graciete wouldn't be staying there.

The living room was Pai's in the afternoons, and eventually, when he snored in the curtained off bedroom, your mother's at night. The TV stood in a corner, and, as you soon discovered with a joy you've rarely felt since, directly reflected MASH, Chiller Theater, and all Ma's favorite Elvis movies onto the rippled glass of the door next to your bed. Awake until she clicked the switch and joined your father behind the curtain, you watched everything she watched, though it all looked like scenes played underwater at the Wilson Avenue pool.

The pool would have been nice right then. It was early May, just after your birthday, but already hot and humid. Graciete seemed not to notice dressed in a dark blue velvet blazer over a white knitted sweater, and matching blue velvet skirt, her black hair in a bun. She looked from you to your mother then stared down the long hallway at Pai, with a look of such intensity that his head suddenly erupted into a burning Cambodian village.

"Mãe, por favor. Please. Don't start. Don't even think about giving her the treatment." Ma sounded tired as she plunked a carrot into a pot of boiling water. "It's different here."

Graciete burned holes in the side of Pai's head for another few minutes.

"Que diferente, que nada! Didn't you ask me to come here? And didn't I come? What's that? Alheira?" Graciete had turned her attention back to Ma and was nodding toward the sausage nestled in butcher paper on top of the refrigerator.
"Não. It's for lunch tomorrow." Ma sounded annoyed like she did when you asked her too many questions.

"For us or him?" Graciete asked.

Ma didn't answer.

You scratched at a scab on your calf until a warm sticky wetness spread on your fingertips.

This was no grandmother. Grandmothers were Grandma Walton saying goodnight to their kin. They were white haired ladies soaking their teeth in a glass of water on the commercial breaks. Graciete hadn't yet smiled so there was no evidence she had her own teeth, but her hair was as black as yours. Grandmothers were ladies who did renda and discussed who had finer twists in the thread, who made the best xailes to wrap around their shoulders at weddings or funerals, while their husbands played malhas in the bocce ball pit in Mosquito Park on Sunday afternoons when the Italians weren't around. Ma called them all "tia." It was confusing.

"Vem," Graciete ordered, taking your hand.

And with that you left the fragrant steam of the kitchen, Ma sliding chicken legs into the boiling pot, Miguel beginning his waking-up whimper. You entered the first car of your train, the foyer that was now Graciete's bedroom. She led you to a suitcase with tape wound around the handle. You leaned closer to read the tag: Graciete da Cruz. Grace of the Cross. Suddenly she was like someone in a movie of the week, walking with a huge cross on her shoulder in one of the festa marches Pai called your mother's village's idea of a good time.

"They broke this open, sure, so they could take what's mine for themselves, but they didn't find this!" From somewhere inside the case or maybe out of thin air Graciete pulled an old sickle, a fouce, with a cracked wooden handle. You knew what it was because Nixon had gone to China, and Ma had recently bought one at Belezas Portuguesas on Ferry St., to weed the strip of dirt behind the garage so she could plant tomatoes and couves. So far it had hung on a nail in the garage, its blade as clean as a crescent moon.

You didn't know much back then but were pretty sure that those white haired ladies on TV never smuggled fouces through customs. They never smuggled mangoes, figs, seeds, plant graftings, or Thanksgiving turkeys either the way Graciete would over the next two decades, traveling back and forth to visit family and renew visas.

She would leave that autumn, in fact, when your parents suddenly decided to move the family to a house across the river, a new start to the same old ends. She would return the following spring, with two pet birds - pintasilgos who flew across the Atlantic tucked in netting from an onion sack that she had sewn into the arms of her coat. They would chirp in the small cage on the kitchen window sill of her two room Pulaski St. apartment, and she would explain, "They just don't have birds with their kind of song in America."

It wouldn't matter that the goldfinch was the state bird of New Jersey.

It still doesn't matter.

"This belonged to my Benedito." Graciete lay the blade of the sickle across her palm. "When they grabbed him in the street and took him away in front of us, all we could do was wait. He didn't know anything, he wasn't one of those students involved in política. We waited and waited."

You didn't understand what she meant. But now you still wonder why some of the renda ladies said things were better when Salazar was alive.

So Benedito must have been your grandfather. You didn't ask. It was one thing to be told so and so emigrated to… It was another thing to want to know. Except for occasional comments, things that slipped in conversations with neighbors or people they ran into on the street or after church - so and so got married or died same thing, my father would say; so and so went to Brazil or France; so and so misstepped and drowned in a well, but that's what you get for drinking too much at the October vindimas - Ma and Pai never talked about who or where they came from.

You sat together quietly on the edge of the bed. "Vamos," she said finally.

You said nothing as she led you out into the late afternoon sun, the aluminum door clanging behind you.

"Mosquito Park, that's not it's real name," you explained, when she finally asked where it was. "It's Independence Park. The city made it for the poor people." You imitated your favorite teacher, Miss Goldsmith, whom Ma called 'That tall Brownie.' "But everyone calls it Mosquito Park."

Graciete walked towards where you had pointed, as if she understood everything you had said. You ran to keep up.

For how many nights you don't know, exactly an hour after dinner, you sat in bath water as hot as you could stand it and watched bits of green, and brown you prayed was only dirt, bobbing over the red crusted sores on your arms and legs. Graciete leaned over the tub scooping water in one of the plastic containers from the Pathmark, empty now of the chicken moelas it had once contained. She alternately hummed and murmured something you couldn't quite understand as she poured the liquid over your head and shoulders. Behind the closed bathroom door your parents' arguing, Miguel's crying, eventually sounded like part of her voice, and the scooping and pouring made the water feel cooler. Afterwards, she dried you, rubbed your arms and legs with alcohol, got you into pajamas and bed.

The chicken pox wasn't incurable after all. But the same way you still long for a middle name, you wish it had been.

Reading Between, Living Beyond
>	Vanessa "Nessa" Acevedo

Abuela,
The little girl in me just wants to hear your stories.
All the ways you kept breathing and walking and
eating and fucking, doing and daring. Tell me why
you abandoned Mami and her brothers and sisters.
Explain to me why you reminded those who took
charge of her to hit her hard if she disobeyed.

Break it down to me how you have dedicated yourself
to witnessing Jehova, writing Mami pages of unabridged
scripture when she only wants to know you, and
especially for you to know her. You constantly warn
her about going to hell. Another version of getting
hit hard if she disobeys. I'm not even mad anymore.
I'm not even trying to travel time and save Mami from
your abandon anymore. I just want to understand your
leg of the journey. I want to recognize the lessons
woven into my DNA. To remember why I was born not
wanting to be touched or told or fucked with. To know
how I didn't trust any male who moved too quickly
towards me without explanation, years before I was
actually violated by a man who turned a hug into a
holding pattern.

I just want to interpret the dreams I have about levitating
over the terrain: a skill I'm sure would have come in useful
to you all those years you starved in the mountains, chased
out of the village by the guerrilleros, beaten by your
resentful padre, raped by soul hungry soldiers, shunned
by an adolescent-unmarried-pregnant-sucia-cualquiera
hating society.

Abuela,

I want my someday children to appreciate why my Mami
was so protective of me. How it is that she held on to me
in the face of both our deaths, looking the doctors trying
to convince her to abort me straight in the eyes, letting
them know in no uncertain terms that her baby wasn't going
anywhere that she was not. Why it is that she never sent me
to church, read me the Bible, mapped out the geography
of Colombia, or taught me about you, her Mamá?

Her lessons instead were modeled dynamics. Morals and ethics,
manners and mentality, seasoning and cumbia, español y poesía.
Things that didn't have the potential to host intentions to
bruise, break, penetrate, humiliate, violate, abandon my precious
body and soul, as had been done to her for so many decades.

Abuela,
I want society to recognize in these narratives:
      The power of love,
           The root of peace,
           The skill of resilience,
           The necessity of compassion,
                      The value of expression,
                      The joy of spirit,
                      The savoring of a meaty life,
                      And palate cleansing of
                              an anointed soul.

Abuela,
They should learn from you that abandon is futile.
How your life of abandon managed to water your seeds with drought.
Mami and I live a life of unquenchable thirst for loving engagement
thanks to you,   and everyone like you,   and everyone not like you.

Tell me your stories so that my own someday children can mark one of
the beginnings of the rest of their lives, footnote their ways through foggy
memories. Find clarity in the difference between surviving
and living, hope and faith, abandon and release.

Abuela,
The little girl in me just wants
to hear your stories
so that the grown woman in me
can chapter and verse
her way towards an epilogue
that will love all us matriarchs
in the voids that were created
by the ways we were once taught
we cannot love ourselves.

Gracias

Mil gracias to Daisy Arroyo who said yes and dedicated many hours to ensuring the photos were exactly what we envisioned. Your talent and work ethic is undeniable. It has been a sincere pleasure and honor to work with you.

Un abrazo fuerte to each model- Olga Huraira Ayala, Elena Mamarazzi Marrero, Tamara G. Saliva, Two Moons Doreen Asia Headen, Maggie Castro Stevens, Addie Diaz-Siverio, Shihan Candy Warixi Soto- Thank you for lending your energy, stories and images to this collection. This would not have been possible without you.

Gratitude goes to each woman writer- Claudia, Nia, Bernice, Rebeca, Maria, PaulA, Alexandra, Vanessa, Shamecca, Annette, Nessa, Karina, Katalina and Warixi. Thank you for giving your fearless voices, truths and talent to this beautiful work of art.

A Special Clap! Clap! Goes to Bernice Sosa for serving as proofreader and making final edits to this beautiful beast! Your late night conversations, suggestions, scanned changes and words of encouragement were essential to the completion of The Abuela Stories Project. Thank you for being brave. I look forward to building mujer!

Kinkamase to The Man of The House Jorge Alvarado (imposible sin ti) tu sabes, yo se-punto.

To my children Shanice, Indio, Nauel and my grandbaby Dyani- you are the reason I create. #letthemcallmyname #letthemfindme #magicmakingisnotforpendejas

Thank you to Kiko Carmelo Dominguez for every email answered and each technical glitch corrected.

Modupe Iya Jacqueline Martin, Iya Linda Evans, Tata Carlos Mora and Ile Odusinya for the growth and guidance.

Gracias to Denise Dominguez for reminding me of the meaning of my name. DD forever!

Gracias to Yoseli Castillo Fuertes for your talent, keen eye and insight!

Un grito fuerte to the entire poetic and artistic community, in the BX and beyond, especially my CantoMundo and Cave Canem Bush Medicine familia, that has shown their love- Ashé

Many thanks to public funds from the Bronx Council on the Arts through the Department of Cultural Affairs' Greater New York Arts Development Fund Program for believing in The Abuela Stories Project.

Biografías de las mujeronas

Peggy Robles-Alvarado is a tenured New York City educator, a CantoMundo, Home School, and Academy for Teachers Fellow as well as a two time International Latino Book Award winner and author of Conversations With My Skin and Homenaje A Las Guerreras/ Homage to the Warrior Women. She is a planning committee member for The Bronx Book Fair and will begin her MFA in Performance and Performance Studies at Pratt Institute fall of 2016. She is a 2014 BRIO performance poet award winner and in 2016 she was named one of the 25 Most Influential Women of the Bronx, a BCA Arts Fund and Spaceworks Bronx Community Artist grant recipient. Her poetry will be included in the forthcoming collection of Afro-Latino Poets published by Arte Publico Press. Peggy has been published in 92Y.org #wordswelivein, NACLA, Letras by the Center for Puerto Rican Studies, The Bronx Memoir Project, The BX Files Anthology, Luna Luna Magazine, Hyperallergic.com, Upliftt.com, Dealmas.net and Sofrito For Your Soul. She has been featured on HBO Habla Women, Lincoln Center Out of Doors, Poets and Writers Fifth Annual Connecting Cultures Reading, and The BADD!ASS Women Festival as well as other culturally notable venues. Determined to build a legacy within the arts, she is continuously creating and supporting literary events and workshops through Robleswrites Productions. For more information please visit Robleswrites.com. or find her on Facebook, Instagram and Twitter @Robleswrites.

Daisy Arroyo is a Bronx artist that evokes visual pleasure and has always found inspiration from her urban roots. Her artistic journey started at an early age in the Sound View Section of the Bronx and has recently flourished in photography where she captures the essence of life and art in unexpected places, shadows, and reflections. Her work has been exhibited in at The Abrons Arts Center as part of the Perspectives from New York City Collection, at The Soho Digital Art Gallery as part of the Springing Through The Lens showcase both premiering spring of 2013. She was also the featured photographer at Canvas of Words: Framing Love, a sold out arts event in Queens in the winter of 2014. Daisy has participated in on location photography shoots at the International Beauty Show at The Jacob Javits Center, at Brooklyn Fashion Weekend, Bronx Fashion Week and various events sponsored by New York Fashion Shows, a company that specializes in showcasing various designers such as Project Runway's winner Irina Shabayeva, Celebrity Designer Michael Costello and Long Champ throughout the year. Most recently, Daisy's keen eye and artistry behind the camera has led her to collaborate with artisans, spoken word artists, and writers from the tri-state area to document the power of words and memory. One of her photographs serves as cover art for The Bronx Memoir Project published by the Bronx Writers Center. To learn more about Daisy Arroyo and her work please contact her at dnova310@aol.com.

Vanessa "Nessa" Acevedo is a Colombian American Artist and Social Worker who aims to serve as a catalyst for therapeutic and authentic expression; exposing her heart, mind, and spirit as an invitation for you to do the same and live to tell about it. Nessa is honored and excited to achieve her first publication in this "Abuela Stories Project". She has been expressing herself through the written word since childhood, breaking through to the open mic in early 2012 at Capicu Culture's: People's Open Mic and going on to perform at open The Nuyorican Poet's Café, Word at 4F, The DoJo, Great Weather for Media's: Spoken Word Sundays, El Fogon, and Smokin' Word and Drum. Nessa can best be reached by e-mail atvacevedo14@yahoo.com.

Nia Andino is a visual artist and writer drawn to elements of visual and verbal expression that reflect the condition of the human soul and the cultural pride of her Caribbean heritage. Nia has shown her artwork at the Aeon Logic Gallery, The Brecht Forum, Center City Galleries, Abrazo Interno Gallery, Alchemist Lounge, Rio II Gallery, the Port Authority Bus Terminal, miLES Gallery, the Chelsea Shul, Victoria Congregational Church and online in SmokeLong Quarterly. She has performed at La Casa Azul bookstore, featured at the Queens NYC Lit Fest and twice at the Nuyorican Poet's Café. She can be reached at andinostyles@gmail.com or through her website at www.andinostyles.com.

Annette Estévez is an NYC poet. She lives in Queens. Or in her head. Or in the questions haunting heartbeats. She's not sure but that's what her poems are for - an endless unraveling. Annette's poetry has been published in the e-journal, Typoetic.us. She has been a featured poet on the web-series BITES, at the NYC Poetry Festival with both Capicu Culture and #growfierce, Bluestockings Bookstore, Cornelia Street Arts Cafe, The Loisaida Center, La Mama Galleria, and Canvas of Words. She was a 2015 recipient of the Butterfly Tribe Scholarship from the School of Poetic Arts (La Sopa). Annette is a mentor at Girls Write Now, an alumna of the 2016 Frost Place Conference on Poetry, and participant in the upcoming Pink Door Writing Retreat. She can be reached via email at estevez.annette@gmail.com.

Vanessa "Chica" Ferreira is the girl with the smile who believes there is strength in vulnerability. Her work can be found in the anthologies "No Apologies" and "Full Circle" published by The Sunday Writing Circle in 2013 and 2014, and in "Letras" for Centro Voices as well as in "The Bronx Files" Contemporary Poetry Written by Bronx Writers published in 2015. She also self-published a poetry collection titled "The Girl With The Smile". Vanessa Chica has featured at various NYC venues such as The Nuyorican Poets Café, The Bronx Museum of the Arts, Urban Juke Joint and The Smokin Word Open Mic Series. She has also performed in The Full Circle Ensemble's From the Page to the Stage, Misconceptions and Misconceptions Too and Mujeres at the Mic at the Association of Writers and Writing Programs in Los Angeles. For more information check out her webpage VanessaChica.com.

Alexandra Hernandez grew up in The Bronx as the eldest daughter of two Puerto Rican parents who always taught her to shoot for the stars and follow her dreams. In college, she wrote a one-act play titled "Bonita" which was directed and performed at the Playwrights Festival at Hunter College and serves as inspiration for one of the pieces in this anthology. Alexandra is currently at work on her first full-length young adult novel, hoping to reach and inspire other young Latinas. She is also an avid salsa dancer, something that she feels strongly influences her work. Hernandez can be contacted at AlexKHernandez87@gmail.com.

Shamecca Long, whose stage name is Nzingha Jane, is a writer and spoken word artist from Brooklyn, NY. Her work has been featured in SIMBAA, thelastwomensmagazine.com, GhettoHeat, Caribbean Life news, and blackcitymag.com. In 2012, she published her self-titled collection of poems "Nzingha Jane." In 2015, after receiving approval from her daughter Saniya Tention, she published "Rainbows" a children's book written by her daughter. She currently blogs for Babymamahood a site dedicated to providing resources, inspiration, and community to unwed mothers from the 'hood. When she's not writing, you can catch her in Brooklyn mentoring high school girls with Young Women Rock! Shamecca Long can be reached at shamecca.long@gmail.com.

Karina Guardiola-Lopez is an author, poet, lyricist, educator and founder of The Pen, The Pad and The Poet series. Her books are available on Amazon, Barnes and Noble and itunes.com. Her work has been published in Poetica Magazine, Tribes Magazine, The Sunday Writing Circle, The Full Circle Ensemble Anthology, La Pluma y La Tina's New Voices, Hostos Community College's English Club Anthology, The City College's Jazz Anthology, The BX Files, Sofritoforyoursoul.com, first writer magazine .com, latinabookclub.com, latinoauthor.com and many others. She is also a member of the Full Circle Ensemble and has performed at two sold out shows at the National Black Theater. For more information please visit www.kglopez.com.

Rebeca Lois Lucret is a writer, poet, memoirist and former contributing writer for Blacktino.net. She is a member of the New York City Latina Writer's Group, The Full Circle Ensemble's Sunday Writing Circle and a Cave Canem alum. She has featured at various NYC venus such as Lit Crawl Brooklyn 2014, The Glitter Pomegranate Performance Series, The Smokin' Word Open Mic Series, Great Weather for Media, The Urban Juke Joint, and Travesías Urbanas/Urban Crossings Poetry Reading. Lucret was a key member of the internationally known world fusion band Machete Movement and was featured in The Full Circle Ensemble's sold out show "From the Page to the Stage" at the National Black Theatre in Harlem. Her poems can be found in Ty(po-e:tic)us Literary Journal, Centro Voices: Letras and The BX Files anthology benefiting El Fogon. Currently Rebeca is working on her memoir "Dandelion Strands" and can be contacted at rebecaloisl@gmail.com.

PaulA Neves, a Canto Mundo fellow, has received scholarships and residencies from the Sundress Academy for the Arts, and the Luso-American Development Foundation. Her writing has most recently appeared in the anthology Writers of the Portuguese Diaspora, Pilgrimage Magazine, Gávea-Brown Journal, Luna Luna Magazine, and Quiddity. Her artwork is featured in the Glassbook Project Collections Provisions, Changed Relationships After 9/11 and Domestic Violence (glassbookproject.org). She is a member of the Kale Soup for the Soul collective (www.facebook.com/KaleSoupfortheSoul/), which has performed nationwide. She can be contacted @itinerantmuse or paulaneves.net

Maria D. Rivas is an educator and writer living in The Bronx who enjoys writing about and discussing education, women, class, race and their intersections. Contact her at mariadrivas1@gmail.com

Katalina Rodriguez is an attorney, musician, poet, curator, community advocate and co-founder of ELKAT Productions. She developed, co-produced and co-directed the "Smokin' Word" LP - a charitable album by world renowned fusion band Machete Movement. She was a featured artist in The Full Circle Ensemble's sold out theater productions From The Page To The Stage and Misconceptions. Rodriguez currently curates "The Smokin' Word Open Mic Series" held monthly in The Bronx. She can be reached at krodriguezesq@yahoo.com.

Bernice Sosa is a second generation Nuyorican Mother, writer, poet, teacher, interpreter and translator from East New York, Brooklyn. She has been published online at Pa'lante Latino, Alexandra Roman's Mink, and El Centro de Estudios Puertorriqueños of Hunter College. Sosa is honored to have shared her work on the stages of Capicu Cultural & Poetry Showcase in Brooklyn, The Nuyorican Poet's Café, La Loba Poetry Series and The Babble in The Bronx. For future work please contact her at bsimom13@gmail.com.

Shihan Candy Warixi Soto is Mother, Grandmother, and Great Grandma. She is a multi- award winning, Hall of Fame High Ranking martial artist and founder of two programs -Secure Your Child and Female Alternative Street Tactics created to empower children and women through self-defense and street awareness. She is an activist, a Taino Spiritual Advisor, as well as the creator of the Taino Awards presently in its eighth year. As a Taino Spiritual Advisor she has been called upon to open and bless many events including The Julia De Burgos Memorial. She is a poet whose most treasured memory is performing at The Nuyorican Poets Café with the late Pedro Pietri. She has been featured in many programs such as Una Noche de Poesia y Musica in memory of the mambo king Tito Puente, Café Largo in a program by Sisters Underground and many other venues. She has been published in Trayectoria Taina and she co-created an annual poetry open mic event in October at Cemi Underground called "The Anti-Columbus Day Smash." Among her many awards she is most proud of Lo Mejor de Nuestra Comunidad given by Comite Noviembre and her Latina 50 Plus 2015 Award. She can be contacted via e mail at Shihan1@optonline.net

Claudia Whittingham aims to be the wildest dream of her ancestors. She is an educator, artist and writer presently living in New York. She has performed her original works as part of African Voices "Let Go" workshops and at Medicine Show Theatre with Rock Wilk. She can be reached at claudianicolewhittingham@gmail.com.

www.ingramcontent.com/pod-product-compliance
Lightning Source LLC
Chambersburg PA
CBHW040058160426
43192CB00003B/103